Charles Bray

The Education of the Feelings

Charles Bray

The Education of the Feelings

ISBN/EAN: 9783741141287

Manufactured in Europe, USA, Canada, Australia, Japa

Cover: Foto ©berggeist007 / pixelio.de

Manufactured and distributed by brebook publishing software
(www.brebook.com)

Charles Bray

The Education of the Feelings

THE
EDUCATION OF THE FEELINGS

A MORAL SYSTEM

REVISED AND ABRIDGED

FOR

SECULAR SCHOOLS.

FOURTH EDITION.

BY CHARLES BRAY.

LONDON:
LONGMANS, GREEN, READER, AND DYER.
1872.

PREFACE.

There exist in all of us certain natural impulses, feelings, or affections, which point to the Duties we have to perform in life. These at present have received no systematical development and training, neither have they at present received proper guidance, so far as regards the community at large. And yet we must *know* what is right in order to *do* what is right. A few moral maxims have been taught, and in order to teach them Religion has hitherto been dragged into the dirt and contaminating influence of our Common Schools, to the injury of Religion and Morality. As Zschokke, the great Swiss Reformer, remarks, "Nothing in the Christian world has so greatly contributed to the decline of Christianity as the reigning practice of imparting the higher ideas of religion to children at an age when their memory only, and not their understanding, is capable of receiving them; and in which a solemn and touching office has been degraded to a merely social custom, mechanically partaken of from habit and decorum."

But whether this be so or not, it is very desirable that in our Common Schools, supported by a common rate, our Duty to God and our Duty to our Neighbour should be taught separately, inasmuch as we can agree as to the latter, but we are all more or less at variance as to what the direct worship and service of God consist in; and surely all our duties in this world may be clearly set forth without mixing them up in any way with duties that belong to a world to come. Children must be taught to do what is right for the love of what is right, and for that alone. We must be careful, however, not to confound moral feeling with moral principle, for in order to do what is right we must know what is true. Hence the necessity for the cultivation of the intellect. But education has hitherto been too exclusively confined to the cultivation of the intellect. The formation of the disposition, or the cultivation of the feelings, is of equal, if not of more importance.

The clearest analysis of our Mental Constitution, both Feelings and Intellectual Faculties, is that presented by Phrenology; and in the previous Editions of this work the Phrenological nomenclature was adopted. This, however, was by no means necessary, and in the present Edition it has not been retained, as the technicality has been found to interfere with the usefulness of the work.

As political power has now been placed in the hands of the majority—that is, of the lowest and most ignorant class, and as they ultimately must rule, it is quite time that a systematic training of the Moral Feelings should begin in our Common Schools.

The questions and answers which have been added to this Edition are not so much for the pupils, as to enable the teachers at once to seize the point of what has been previously laid down. The teacher also will be expected to furnish illustrations of the duties inculcated, since little more than principles can be expected in a small work like the present. Mr. Samuel Smiles' books on "Character," "Self Help," &c., will be found useful for this purpose. If teachers in this way carefully prepare such lessons, they may be made the most interesting, as well as the most valuable of the daily course.

COVENTRY, Oct., 1872.

CONTENTS.

PART I.

The Duties we owe to Ourselves:

Feelings that aid in the Estimate we form of Ourselves, and induce us to seek Applause of Others:

PART II.

SOCIAL FEELINGS.

Our Duties to Parents, Brothers and Sisters, Friends:

PART III.

THE MORAL FEELINGS.

PART IV.

PART V.

PART VI.

THE EDUCATION OF THE FEELINGS.

Our Feelings consist of those that induce us to take care of ourselves—the Self-Protecting; those that aid in the estimate we form of ourselves and induce us to seek the applause of others—the Self-regarding; those which unite us to our family and friends—the Social; those which unite us to our fellow-creatures—the Moral; those which regard the Arts and Poetry—the Æsthetic; and some which offer equal aid to all.

To complete our Mental Constitution, we must add the Senses and the Intellect which are required for the proper guidance of these Feelings.

The object of Moral Training is the full development of each Feeling: to cultivate those that are weak, to restrain those which are too strong, and thus to produce a full and harmonious action of the mind.

PART I.

THE DUTIES WE OWE TO OURSELVES; FOR UNLESS WE TAKE CARE OF OURSELVES WE CAN DO NOTHING FOR OTHERS.

FOOD AND HEALTH.

Appetite.—We must eat to live, not live to eat. Unless we did eat we could not live, and nature has made the Duty very pleasant to us; and more than that, for if in the busy turmoil of life we forgot what is of so much importance, our attention is called to it by the pains of hunger. The pleasures of appetite, however, are so great that it is probable there is much suffering from over-eating. This often arises from mismanagement in early life. Eating something nice is too often made the reward for good conduct, and children from the earliest infancy are pacified by something to eat. A child cries, and it is soothed by something eatable—a convenient resource for keeping it quiet; or it is naughty, and it is promised something nice if it will behave well; and often, worse still, it is promised without fulfilment, for a broken promise has a worse effect than hunger or the stomach-ache. Is it wonderful, then, that in after life the importance of the pleasures of appetite should be over-rated?

Children should be early taught politeness in the Johnsonian sense—in giving no preference to themselves; and should learn to take the smallest pieces and the least inviting, and leave the best for others.

Food should be plain, varied, and taken at regular intervals, and with children those intervals should not be too long. With rapidly-growing children the diet should be generous and plentiful.* We should all eat

* "How it was even possible for scientific men to forget that a child *not merely lives but grows*, I cannot guess; but without wasting more breath than is necessary for one hearty imprecation on the stupidity of some of our ancestors in this respect, let me implore every one present to do his part to establish it as an unquestionable rule of practice, that (with proper attention to obvious matters as to its quality) the food of children up to, and especially during, the trying period of sexual development, should be practically unlimited except by the limits of appetite, or the occurrence of positive and unmistakable failure of primary digestion."—*Dr. Francis E. Anstie*, "*The Journal of Mental Science*," *January*, 1872, *p.* 480.

slowly, and if we do so the appetite will generally be a correct measure of quantity. Children should be taught that it is wrong to eat till they are uncomfortable or stupid, and much will depend in this respect on the habits of early life.

Irregularity in meals, and sweetmeats and other delicacies between times, weaken and disorder the stomach; and parents must not suppose that the mischief stops there: the disorder rises to the head, for there is a strong sympathy between the stomach and the moral feelings. The acerbity of one often comes from the acidity of the other—a sour disposition from a sour stomach. Temper often comes from indigestion, and a good digestion is frequently all that is wanted to make the temper bright and cheerful. The dark side that some people always see in life often arises from a digestion ruined in childhood, or from the injudicious practice of taking physic in forgetfulness of what Voltaire says—that the practice of medicine is putting that of which we know little into a body of which we know less. With much cake, sweetmeats, pastry, must always go a large allowance of rod; and Dr. William Sweetser says "an exclusive diet of bread and milk, united with judicious exercise in the open air, will often prove the most effectual means of correcting the temper of peevish and refractory children."

HEALTH.—Although a sound mind and a sound body necessarily go together, yet the "Laws of Health" do not properly come under Moral training.*

* We refer the reader to Mrs. Charles Bray's "Physiology for Schools," in which these Laws are clearly and concisely laid down without that technicality which has hitherto made the subject inadmissible into early education.

Question. Why is it necessary to take care of ourselves?

Answer. Because without health and strength we could not properly perform our other duties.

Q. Why do we eat?

A. We eat to live, not live to eat.

Q. What should we eat, and when?

A. Our food should be plain and wholesome, varied, plentiful, and taken at regular intervals, and these intervals, or the time between meals, with children, should be short.

Q. Why is it necessary that these things should be constantly attended to?

A. Because the health suffers if they are not, and with the health the temper and disposition—acerbity goes with acidity, a sour disposition with a sour stomach.

COURAGE, LOVE OF OPPOSITION, SELF-DEFENCE.

The earliest form of animal life is an animal all stomach; to this is immediately added a power of self-defence, which ultimately develops into what we call Courage—a desire to overcome opposition and meet difficulties.

The world is full of difficulties and danger, and we should get on very badly without Courage, so that where it is naturally deficient we must do all we can to cultivate it. In early childhood the deficiency of this love of opposition is felt to be a happy circumstance: the child is docile and tractable, takes a suggestion immediately, does as he is bid, has no will of his own. Cause for congratulation, however, lessens every year. The least trifles discourage; at lesson-time you are wearied with the constant whining, "I can't do it;" and at play-time you are mortified to see one pursuit after another abandoned at the slightest difficulty. The boy wants courage and manly spirit to encounter and overcome. It is impossible, however, to attain eminence in any active direction in the world without it. We must constantly encourage the child, therefore, to meet and overcome obstacles without our aid, and never let him rest satisfied to leave anything half finished. Dangers and difficulties must be daily created. Riding, climbing, and even hunting may be resorted to for this purpose. We must not hide danger, or always guard children from it by our power and experience, but teach them to meet it boldly. Let them know the consequences to be incurred, and the pain to be borne, and teach them to bear it. Courage consists in meeting danger, not in blindly overlooking it. The most mischievous results may often be witnessed from surrounding children—boys especially—from their earliest infancy with those whose duty is made to consist in doing everything for them, in guarding them from every little danger and inconvenience, clearing every path and obstruction, and constantly coddling and waiting upon them, instead of teaching them to meet and overcome all their little difficulties themselves, and occasionally helping them to do so. Under such mistaken kindness this faculty becomes frequently paralysed, and all is done that can be done to make a puny, puling, weak, effeminate character.

But sometimes we have the feeling in excess; it then requires directing and restraining. The best method is to find the feeling a legitimate course for action in pursuits that we approve, and to let it spend itself upon the difficulties there to be encountered. But it often takes the form of opposition for its own sake, and it then requires very delicate management. We must bear in mind that the exhibition of any feeling in one person is calculated to arouse the same feeling in others, and this sympathy is much stronger than is generally admitted. In children especially the outward expression of another's mind is reflected as in a mirror. In correcting a child this fact should never be lost sight of. If our tone is harsh and captious, the child's feelings will at once be arrayed against the reproof, instead of softened into contrition. The reflection from ourselves is so instantaneous that it is sometimes hard to say on which side the discipline is first and most needed. A mother sees her child doing something wrong; in a sharp angry tone she desires him to desist immediately. The child's disposition to oppose is roused by the tone of the reproof, and he still persists; upon which the mother repeats the command still more sharply—perhaps adding a threat by way of enforcing it. This also is often disregarded, as is every succeeding attempt to procure obedience, because the child's love of opposition is sure to be excited in proportion to the mother's. If the child is deterred by force or punishment, he will do the same thing again when his mother is not present, because he has no motive but fear to prevent him. "Do as you would be done by" would throw light on many a dilemma of this kind, and suggest the right course in multitudes of cases where no other general rule can be applied. Put yourself as much as possible in the child's place. Picture to yourself the kind of admonition that would have the most power over your own mind—the tone of voice and manner that could least excite passion and rouse opposition, and adopt that. Do not attempt to drive, but always to lead. When a child is interested in some object of his own do not, by a sudden command, interfere with it, but rather allow him a few minutes' grace, and gradually divert his attention from one thing to another. Do not unnecessarily thwart children in their little objects; for however insignificant they are to you, they are all-important to them, and pursued with proportionate eagerness. The temper of no child is proof, or ought to be proof, against the frequent, useless intermeddling of some parents and nurses, by whom he is allowed to bring nothing to an end, and obliged to relinquish all his little projects uncompleted. The more a child possesses of the spirit of opposition, the more uniformly kind and considerate should its instructors be.

But Courage, both physical and moral, must be at the base of every manly character. The deficiency, rather than the excess, is therefore most to be deprecated, however difficult it may be to deal with that excess in early life.

The love of contention and opposition for their own sake constitutes the abuse of the faculty; the proper management of it, therefore, when in excess, evidently consists in exciting its direct manifestation as little as possible. By the force of sympathy, the manifestation of Combativeness in one person immediately arouses the feeling in another.

Q. Why do we require Courage?

A. Because the world is full of difficulties and dangers which it is necessary to overcome.

Q. Why should children not be perpetually helped out of their difficulties?

A. Because it weakens their Courage, and their own love and power to meet such dangers and difficulties and to overcome them.

Q. How are unreasonable contention and opposition best met?

A. By kindness and reason. Contention only begets contention, and opposition opposition.

ANGER AND PASSION, AND ENERGY OF CHARACTER.

There is a feeling within us which makes us wish to give pain to those who give pain to us, and for the time at least to hate them; and, as Shakespeare has put into the mouth of Shylock, "Hates any man the thing he would not kill?" But this is a feeling that requires restraint; as the Apostle says, "Be ye angry and sin not;" and if not restrained it leads on to hatred, malice, and all uncharitableness,—to passion, revenge, and cruelty. It was thought "by them of old time" that there should be an eye for an eye and a tooth for a tooth—that so much suffering should always be apportioned to so much sin, and this exact retaliation was dignified by the names of "responsibility" and "righteous retribution." But we live under a different dispensation, and we know now that no more suffering should ever be inflicted than is sufficient to prevent a repetition of the offence. The expression of this feeling of Anger in petty revenge is often foolishly encouraged by nurses: "Did the naughty stick fall down and hurt baby?—*beat* naughty stick!" and even if a brother or sister is the offender, the same amiable spirit of retaliation is impressed. A lady once trod inadvertently on the toes of a little cherub-faced girl; she pursued her like a fury, and would not be appeased till she had stamped on her toes in return; and parents themselves frequently punish their children on the same principle for an involuntary error, provided its consequences are vexatious to themselves. The tone of correction in general partakes too much of passion and the spirit of revenge rather than of sorrow and of love. While this is the case we cannot expect children to learn to subdue the irritation of temper they feel when anything displeases them, and the habit once formed of giving way to it will be most difficult of subjection in after life. When with an excess of this feeling there is a considerable love of opposition in a child, the temper becomes extremely difficult to manage, and perhaps the only way to succeed is to avoid as much as possible all occasions of exciting it, so that the feeling may decrease for want of exercise; while at the same time we cultivate diligently the moral and reasoning powers to oppose it. Even in the cradle the discipline should be begun: everything that is liable to excite the temper, to arouse the irascible feelings, should as far as possible be avoided, and when once excited, instead of leaving the child to cry and wear its passion out, its attention should be diverted and its feelings changed. From want of proper caution in small instances like this, a child frequently begins life with a bias in the temper and disposition not easily to be remedied. Our great aim should be not to rouse a passion, for when once aroused passion cannot be suddenly stopped, but must have a certain sway. The great desideratum *then* is to give it as harmless a direction as possible. If a harmless direction can be found, it is better that a child should have its anger and ill-temper out than that it should remain to breed ill-humours in the mind.

We should never give unnecessary pain to any creature, and certainly never inflict pain for the sake of pleasure to ourselves. If children were properly brought up in love and sympathy with all around, what is called "sport" would be no sport to them: there would be no pleasure in killing even what we require for our daily food. Battues on poor half-tame pheasants, pigeon shootings and other such "sports," are only evidence of the semi-barbarous age in which we live.

The love of mischief seems to arise partly from this propensity and partly from the want of proper occupation for a restless, active spirit. Let children have plenty of useful and innocent employment found for them, and they will not be so fond of exercising their faculties to the destruction of things around them.

This feeling, like all others, is most readily caught from sympathy; and in an atmosphere of kindness and justice it is most easily controlled and soonest declines.

Where this feeling is deficient it often marks a great want of energy in the character; and the feeling cannot be too strong when it takes the direction of indignation against all wrong, and anger against all that is dirty and mean.

Q. Should we wish to give pain to those who have given pain to us, or who have otherwise injured us?

A. No; if they have done wrong we should take exactly that course that is most likely to make them see that they have done wrong, and so to prevent it in future.

Q. Is it not right, then, always to punish wrong-doing?

A. Punishment is never right if a fault can be corrected without, and no more punishment should ever be given than is sufficient to correct a fault, and to prevent its repetition in the future.

Q. Ought we ever to have pleasure in giving pain?

A. No; therefore all killing for sport is wrong.

Q. How is the love of mischief in children best controlled?

A. By plenty of useful and healthy occupation.

Q. When is it right to be angry?
A. We should be angry and indignant against all wrong, oppression, and tyranny, and against all that is dirty and mean.

OPENNESS AND RESERVE—CUNNING.

The mind may be said almost as much to require a covering as the body, and we have a natural feeling of Reserve by which this is accomplished. We must never tell anything but the truth as far as we know it, but still "the truth is not to be told *at all times.*" It is better to suppress our thoughts and feelings when their expression would make mischief and give useless pain to others. There are many other occasions on which a prudent reserve only shows a due discretion, but their full consideration may be well left till later in life. In childhood it is desirable to cultivate an open, candid, truthful disposition.

It is necessary clearly to see the young mind in all its inmost workings as well as outward manifestations, in order to direct it aright. A child should therefore repose unlimited confidence in one or both of his parents; and that he may be encouraged to this, fear should be banished from the intercourse; the child should learn to look upon them as sympathising friends who will enter into all his feelings and enjoyments, and to whom he may freely communicate his thoughts upon all occasions. They will thus be able to give the right direction to the feelings and propensities, and uproot error before its growth shall have injured, as all error must do, the truths already planted. It is scarcely credible to those who have not minutely observed it, to what a train of errors one false perception will give rise in the mind of a child. A French author justly observes on this subject, "Error, dangerous in itself, is still more so by propagation: one produces many. Every man compares more or less his ideas together. If he adopt a false idea, that united with others produces such as are necessarily false, which combining again with all those which his memory contains, gives to all of them a greater or less tinge of falsehood." Again he says, "A single error is sufficient to degrade a people, to obscure the whole horizon of their ideas." These errors can only be properly removed at their source, which is not easily discovered unless children are in the habit of confiding closely in their instructor; if he be a judicious one he will not despise their little ideas, nor ridicule their mistakes or simple misapprehensions.

A child who was very literal in his ideas had often heard the passage of Scripture read, "Even the very hairs of your head are all numbered," and received from it the idea that a figure denoting its particular number was inscribed on each hair. One day his brothers and sisters were amusing themselves with a microscope, and called him eagerly to look through it at a few hairs placed underneath. He looked at it earnestly for some time, and then muttered, "I don't see the number!" His companions laughed at the absurdity of his exclamation. He was abashed at their laughter, and did not explain, but the idea remained in his mind that the Bible had said what was not true.

It is the mistaken idea of some parents that in order to secure the confidence of their children, they must assume a sort of infallibility, and never let it be found out that their own knowledge is at fault. When therefore they are taxed with questions that they cannot answer they evade them by such prevarications as "Want of time just then to attend to them,"—"Not a proper question to be asked,"—"Beyond a child's capacity to understand,"—and so on. Such parents little think how much they undermine confidence by this and every species of shuffling, which children are sure to detect and almost as sure to imitate. It is their duty to qualify themselves in every possible way for satisfying the desire for knowledge in their children; but if they cannot, let them simply and honestly confess their ignorance, and become fellow-learners with their children to find an answer, if the question is worth answering. A half-educated mother, who pretends to no more knowledge than she really has, but who has the wish for more, commands much more the respect and confidence of her children than if her learning and acquirements were the bluest possible, because they know that what she professes to know she really does know, and because it is the instinct of humanity from childhood upwards to respect and confide in truth and honesty far more than in extent of knowledge. It is the same with moral deficiencies. Parents know that they ought to be models for their offspring, and sometimes therefore wish it to be assumed that they are so, and tacitly forbid their own weaknesses being made subject of comment before the children. The little creatures, however, make comments enough about them amongst themselves, and perhaps learn that hypocrisy is a grace for the drawing room, and truth a luxury for the nursery. Perfect candour towards our children with respect to our own failings,—showing that we earnestly desire to correct them if we can, and if we cannot, using them as a warning for their benefit,—is the best possible way of making them candid and above all disguise in return.

Where real confidence exists between parents and their child, there is little danger to be apprehended even from a naturally too reserved disposition, because the parents will be able to see its workings, and counteract them where they are tending to evil. They will encourage the confession of faults by leniency, and prove to the offender that openness is more advantageous than concealment. When a child with such a disposition is treated with severity or indifference, when his thoughts and feelings, if he does utter them, are disregarded, when the avowal of a fault draws down the chastisement instead of averting it, what can we expect but that he should use cunning to attain his wishes, and falsehood to evade punishment? If deceit and lying be made his interest, he will practise them.

The summary modes of punishment still in frequent use, such as corporeal punishment, solitary confinement, or tasks for all species of misconduct, have a strong tendency to call deceit and cunning only into exercise. Children not seeing the connection between the penalty and the offence, naturally enough conclude that to avoid the former they have only to conceal the latter. The proper punishment for a fault is the natural consequences of the error. We should, therefore, in order to correct a fault, allow these natural consequences, when not too heavy, to fall upon the child, who will thus generally see the connection between them, and abstain from its commission in future; but when these consequences are not plainly discernible, or are too remote to operate sufficiently, the punishment should have reference to the offence. For example, he is permitted to play in a garden upon condition that he wilfully damages nothing; he tramples down the young and tender plants to reach the unripe fruit, which he plucks—the natural consequence is the loss of the flowers and fruit in their season. But he has also broken the condition on which he was admitted—the punishment for this is exclusion from the privilege, until a sincere conviction of his error vouches for his better fulfilment of the condition. Or, in a fit of passion, he may have hurt or injured his companions—the natural punishment is the being left by them until the state of mind which induced the commission of the fault is changed, and he seeks their society and forgiveness, sensible of his own error in alienating those whose companionship is necessary to his happiness. The only proper and effectual remedy for error is to show why it is error, and to excite the desire to correct it; merely to forbid it under certain penalties, without this conviction of the understanding, rather induces the child to commit it, when he can do so with impunity.

As motives to obedience, the selfish feelings should be appealed to as little as possible, even in early childhood; and when the moral feelings have been cultivated and strengthened, not in any case. Thus we should not appeal to a child's appetite, or his fear, to his desire of applause, or pride; but to his sense of right, his desire to make us happy, his love and veneration for God, from whom, as he may soon be taught to perceive, all his enjoyments proceed.

What we have to aim at is a prudent reserve, where the feelings shall be restrained with a proper regard to time, place and circumstance. An open, frank, ingenuous disposition is the most lovely of all, and that to which we can the soonest attach ourselves; but it does not always follow that a child of reserved temper is disingenuous; love of truth, candour of spirit, and a warm affectionate disposition may dwell under the natural reserve. Kindness and trust will cherish and draw forth the best feelings of such a nature, while severity and suspicion will act upon it with most baneful influence.

A sound writer observes, "There is nothing that we ought to reject with more unalterable firmness than an action that, by its consequences, reduces us to the necessity of duplicity and concealment. No man can be eminently respectable, or amiable, or useful, who is not distinguished for the frankness and candour of his manners. This is the grand fascination by which we lay hold of the hearts of our neighbours, conciliate their attention, and render virtue an irresistible object of imitation."

There are two classes of character with which we are all more or less familiar—those whose feelings and emotions may all be said to go on outside of them, and those who keep all their thoughts and feelings to themselves. We are drawn at once to the frank, candid, open-hearted person, but our love is perhaps more lasting for the prudently reserved. We dislike loud expression even where the virtues are alone concerned, and the reserved person is much less likely to offend in all other respects than the open one. We hold the clear light of truth to be desired above everything, but the close person will frequently find his account in his reserve, as the world often gives credit for sense where there is only silence, and believes a well to be deep when it is only dark. A sanguine temperament with little natural reserve leads to great loquacity, and often betrays short-comings against which there would be no other than this self-witness.

CUNNING.—Some children, who are not otherwise untruthful, have a natural love of attaining their ends by indirect courses: they prefer conquering by stratagem to open force. The proper course with such children is carefully to watch and expose all their little artifices, to show their futility, and how much more manly a simple, straightforward course would be. They do not like to be found out, soon get ashamed, and often mend.

Q. What disposition is most admirable?

A. A candid and truthful one.

Q. Is the truth to be spoken at all times?

A. No, because by so doing we should often give unnecessary pain; but we are never to say what is not the truth under any circumstances.

Q. What is a secret?

A. That which has been entrusted to us in confidence by another; that which the person who has told us would not wish to have known; or which if known would bring scandal or useless trouble upon some one else.

Q. Are we bound to keep a secret?

A. We may be as open as we please about our own affairs, but a secret is not our own property, since it has been entrusted to us by another, and therefore is not ours to part with. We should not, however, accept secrets which must be kept from those who have *a right* to our confidence.

INDUSTRY, THRIFT, PROVIDENCE AND IMPROVIDENCE, INDEPENDENCE AND SELF-RELIANCE.

Industry.—Why does civilised man instinctively feel that Industry is one of the foremost of the virtues, and one to be most sedulously cultivated from early youth?

Buddha made the aim of life to be eternal rest. Christ, with a truer insight, made work here and work hereafter to be the highest destiny of man. "Ye have been faithful in a few things, I will make you ruler over many things. Enter ye into the joy of your Lord." And the more man progresses the more he finds that the exercise of all the faculties, the perpetual search after good, is the highest good.

We naturally desire Happiness; but what is Happiness? The Greenlander's heaven is to sit round an ever-boiling cauldron of whale-blubber; the Buddhist's heaven is cold, passionless Nirwana. To the more advanced minds happiness is not in having, but in obtaining:

> "No endeavour is in vain;
> Its reward is in the doing,
> And the rapture of pursuing
> Is the prize the vanquished gain."—*Longfellow.*

J. Stuart Mill defines a happy life to be "an existence made up of few and transitory pains, many and various pleasures, with a decided predominance of the active over the passive, and having as the foundation of the whole, not to expect more from life than it is capable of bestowing." Mde. de Stael defines happy life to be, "Constant occupation for a desirable object, with a sense of continual progress." Nathaniel

Hawthorne says, "There is no use of life but just to find out what is fit for us to do; and doing it, it seems to be little matter whether we live or die in it."

If we conclude, as perhaps we may, that happiness is harmony of our nature with surrounding conditions, we know that this harmony or equilibrium can only be attained, like the equilibrium of the planetary bodies, through perpetual motion. Rest is fatal to it. Let man rest inert, and the equilibrium is presently destroyed by a dominating feeling or physical want.

Happiness thus becomes more possible as man becomes more developed. What was the source of pure terror to the savage, is the element of the sublime to the cultivated; and education, progress, civilisation, are so many terms to indicate the increased amount of enjoyable existence obtained by the awakening of the latent powers into sympathetic action with surrounding conditions. Hence, to make self the principal object of our regard, and idle, sensual enjoyment the chief aim of life, is to limit those powers, and to destroy all possibility of the greatest happiness. The wider range a man has for his faculties—the more he lives and works for others besides himself, the more happiness-producing power he has. Thus, to teach a child to find daily some useful work to do, and especially work for others, must be one of the first lessons in earliest life.

Industry is the effect of habit, and requires teaching and forming like other habits. It is most important, since constant occupation induces the most healthy frame of mind, and is the foundation of success in all departments. In the division of labour and in the great accumulation of its fruits—that is, of Capital—it is forgotten that a man who consumes more than he produces is living at some other's expense; and it is time we began to inquire at whose expense it is. We have to "learn and labour truly to get our own living," but in the present day, when machinery does so much of the work, we ought not to require to devote our whole time to it, as that can only be at the expense of the higher part of our nature; and it is by his manhood, not by his money, that a man must be measured.

People in the present day live too much to get rich. Love, truth, and beauty, music and poetry, nature and art—these are the highest objects of existence; but these are sacrificed, and the greater part of life spent in acquiring riches, merely that we may eat, drink, sleep, clothe, and ride luxuriously, and otherwise lead the life of a mere animal. Young people should be early taught the real objects of life, that they may not lose its end in acquiring the means; that it is within ourselves that the springs of happiness must arise, and not in any external advantages; and the means of gratifying all the highest requirements of our nature God has made as plentiful as pure air and water.

Thrift.—But the great majority of the people in the world now have to work hard to get a living, and fortunately a "living" now includes the comforts as well as the necessaries of life. To all, whether they are getting much or little, it is desirable to teach the necessity for saving. We must never consume all our earnings: something must be left to fall back upon against the rainy day. This Thrift is the foundation of almost all other virtues among the labour class. There can be no provident forethought without it, no independence, no self-reliance. Without something laid by, sickness or temporary want of work may spoil all a man's wisely laid plans for the future, and he may begin to rely upon others rather than upon himself; and this will inevitably be his first step downwards—the beginning of a moral degradation. The Charities of the present day have too great a tendency to sap this forethought, self-reliance, and self-respect, by teaching the poor to expect to reap where they have not sown, and of those who are thus taught to rely upon Doles and Charities rather than upon their own efforts and savings, two out of three, at least, are disappointed, with the worst possible result both upon character and circumstances; for the great element in all providence is certainty.

TECHNICAL EDUCATION.—As it is necessary in after life that we should all work—should produce and accumulate, so in childhood all should be taught the full use of their hands. Employment is necessary to the health of both body and mind, and children should be taught *how* to occupy themselves. Persons who teach music, the piano for instance, know how desirable it is that their pupils should begin early to use the keys, as their fingers then acquire a facility which cannot be attained in after life; in the same manner children, if properly assisted and instructed, gain a mechanical dexterity of infinite service to them in almost all the pursuits of life, and which might very much lessen the necessary term of apprenticeship to any manual employment. When this facility in the use of the fingers is not acquired early, and when the natural disposition to it is deficient, it can seldom be afterwards attained, and an inaptitude for all manual operations will be conspicuous through life. Building houses, bridges, &c., with wooden bricks, or with cards, joining dissected maps, cutting figures in paper, drawing, are all useful exercises towards the acquisition of this facility, and therefore useful in-door amusements; but it should be borne in mind that children are always happier when a pleasant employment to themselves is also of use to their elders, and they will work with great alacrity at it if their attention be not confined too long. As boys grow older, the juvenile workshop will become an excellent school for the propensity.

In all ranks, power and skill in the use of the hands are most desirable. Vacant minutes and hours may then be filled up with useful and agreeable occupation which would otherwise be devoted to listlessness and ennui, and the mind is refreshed for renewed exertion. When the mind has been over-excited or disturbed, manual occupation tranquilises it, and restores its equilibrium, when study would only increase the evil. In the tedium of sickness its assistance is invaluable, by gently drawing off the attention from the languid and uneasy bodily feelings which accompany the lighter degrees of suffering.

The needle and its kindred labours are the never-failing resource of the one sex; the pencil, the tool-box, the chemical apparatus, and many other implements of art or science, will furnish the other with useful and interesting employment in the intervals of more important avocations, or of mental labours.

Q. Why should we be industrious?
A. Because the greatest happiness is found in constant occupation in the path of duty.
Q. What are the highest objects of existence?
A. The True, the Good, and the Beautiful, and these must not be sacrificed that we may grow rich, for a man is measured by his manhood, and not by his money.
Q. Is it desirable to save?
A. Yes; we should never spend all our earnings, because without such provident forethought there is no provision against misfortune, no independence, no self-reliance. In paying our debts we are not "squandering away" our money, for as the proverb says, "He who pays his debts does not thereby grow poorer."
Q. Is it desirable that we should learn to use our hands early?
A. Yes, because by such use greater facility may be attained and much time spared in after life, when possibly such facility could not be attained at all.

CAUTION, DISCRETION, PRUDENCE, CIRCUMSPECTION.

These virtues all arise in the same feeling of Fear, which in excess leads to timidity and cowardice. Our care must be that one does not run into the other. The better part of valour is discretion. We cultivate and admire Courage, and in a world so full of difficulties and dangers, in public estimation it has taken precedence of Discretion; but it is quite as necessary to avoid danger as to fight with that which must be met. It is difficult in education always to draw the line, public opinion unduly favouring bravery; but a manly character will combine both courage and disertion, and the moral courage that does decline the combat where fighting is wrong and discretion the right course, is the highest feeling.

Before children understand the nature of the objects around them they have reason to be cautious, and therefore in them the feeling usually predominates. Education must step in to prevent caution from degenerating into timidity, and its deficiency from giving rise to heedlessness. If a child be heedless, the most effectual method of cure, when it can be adopted without serious mischief ensuing, is to let him feel fully the consequences of his rashness. If he will put his hand too near the fire, let him be burnt; if he will over-balance himself, let him fall down; if he will tease the cat, let her scratch him; and these self-taught lessons will make a more lasting impression than many a prudent warning or angry admonition. On the other hand, children who are naturally timid are frequently made cowards by the injudicious care and attention of those around. For example, the child, in attempting to run alone, stumbles and falls down; the whole family start up alarmed, anxious inquiries and ejaculations are poured into the child's ears, until he begins to find out, what he would scarcely have known otherwise, that he has been hurt. Then begins a roar, and then are redoubled the expressions of commiseration, and meanwhile the child thinks to himself, "What a perilous adventure! What a little hero I was to tumble down!" A thousand unheeded bruises would do him less harm than the ill-timed sympathy. From having every trifling mishap made a matter of such prodigious importance he will soon learn to consider pain a mighty evil, and his own pain especially to be lamented and guarded against, and will perhaps grow up one of those selfish, calculating persons who never can persuade themselves to do a good action without being first morally certain that not the slightest inconvenience will be thereby entailed upon themselves. We do not mean to say that children are to be treated with unkindness and neglect; but it is truer kindness to try to render the mind superior to pains and trials than to let such pains and trials get the mastery.

But there is more to be feared from excessive timidity than from too great rashness; we should therefore be careful to give this feeling as little stimulant, as little exercise as possible—for every feeling is strengthened by exercise and weakened by inactivity. Children can no more help feeling afraid than they can help feeling the tooth-ache. It is absurd, therefore, and very injudicious only to laugh at their fears, unless a cheerful laugh will help to dispel them and restore confidence. We ought to protect children as much as possible from imaginary fears until they are of an age to see their groundlessness, and until other feelings have acquired sufficient strength to supply moral courage. Feelings are aroused more by sympathy with others than by precept and lectures; particularly is fear caught from what is seen of the feeling manifested by those about us. Richter says, "One scream of fear from a mother may resound through the whole life of her daughter; for no rational discourse can extinguish the mother's scream."* Early fears have nothing to do with reason, and are to be treated as we would treat a bodily ailment. However unreasonable their fears, do not force children to bear them: show their groundlessness if

* "Levana, or the Doctrine of Education."

possible, and accustom them to objects of terror by degrees. Never let us judge of their state of mind by our own. We say this equally with reference to all the feelings, for in no case are the feelings of a child and of a grown-up person alike. This too common mistake of judging children by ourselves is productive of infinite error and wrong. Timidity, over-caution, indecision, arise from the excess of cautiousness, and such weaknesses are incompatible with greatness, or even with success in any high object.

Q. Is it desirable to be Cautious?

A. Yes, the better part of valour is discretion, and it is often more prudent to avoid danger than to court it. Prudence and Caution are often the same. In early life Caution is our great protection against the necessary ignorance of the nature of everything that surrounds us.

Q. What is Fear?

A. Caution in excess, and where it exists children should be trained to meet danger and difficulty, and carefully to discriminate between real and fictitious danger.

Q. Should we laugh at Fear, and be angry with children for being afraid?

A. With many children fear is natural and cannot be avoided, and it would be quite as reasonable to laugh at them, or be angry with them, for having the tooth-ache. Its expression, however, may be controlled, and it will get less, although it may not cease to exist, as children grow older.

Q. Ought we to be careful not to show fear before children?

A. It is one of the strongest feelings in our nature, and caught perhaps more than any other by sympathy; we ought therefore carefully to restrain our own unreasonable fears.

THE LOVE OF LIFE AND FEAR OF DEATH.

Whatever people may sometimes say, they have a great love of life for its own sake, and for the happiness which it gives them; but there is in our nature beyond this a feeling which produces an instinctive wish to preserve life for its own sake, independently of the pleasure or pain with which it may be accompanied. It induces men to cling to life in circumstances in which otherwise existence might not be thought desirable. This instinctive feeling it is which perhaps, more than reason or principle, prevents men escaping from temporary suffering by suicide. It is this feeling, assisted by Faith and Hope, which has, in all countries, originated the idea of a future state. Little can be said here with reference to the education of the feeling, although we must refer to the mischief which results from the too common mode of treating the subject of death. Death is as natural as Birth, and ought to be as painless, but all the fictitious horrors possible have been accumulated round it from erroneously conceived moral purposes. It has been made a bugbear to frighten people into behaving well, very little to the interests of morality, but greatly to the loss of happiness of all concerned, particularly to timid children. The representations of death itself in pictures, and in pictures too that are given to children for their amusement, are of a hideous and revolting kind. The accompanying circumstances of death, churchyards, sepulchres, and coffins, are associated in their minds with dreariness, gloom, and superstitious horrors. "A child came running into its mother's room one day, sobbing violently, 'Mamma, Mamma, I don't like to die; all the dirt will get into my eyes!" This childish fear is perhaps not more erroneous than the common view taken by "children of a larger growth."

George Eliot says, "When the commonplace 'We

must all die' transforms itself suddenly into the acute consciousness 'I must die—and soon,' then death grapples us, and his fingers are cruel; afterwards he may come to fold us in his arms as our mother did, and our last moment of dim earthly discerning may be like the first." *

"To fancy, as many do, that death is not only terrible and affrighting, but physically powerful, is quite a mistake, being to look for sensibility in the *loss* of sensibility. Death is a sleep rather than a sensation; a suspension of our faculties rather than a conflict with them: instead of a time of suffering, a time of deepening unconsciousness. Dr. Baillie tells us that his observation of death-beds inclines him to the firm belief that 'nature intended we should go out of the world as unconsciously as we came into it.'" † The consequence of the injudicious representations so frequently made is the great dread of death that sometimes embitters the whole of life; the only antidote to which feeling is the faith which enables us to place our ultimate fate, with unbounded confidence, in the hands of our Creator.

Q. What is the Love of Life?

A. A strong feeling which makes us desire to live, whether, for the time, we are happy or miserable; it prevents suicide, and makes us wish for continued existence.

Q. How has the idea of a Future Life originated in all countries?

A. In the instinctive promptings of this feeling, and in the wish to rejoin the friends we have lost by death.

Q. What is Death?

A. The natural termination of our existence here.

* "Middlemarch," vol. 2, p. 370.

† "Life: its Nature, Varieties, and Phenomena," p. 278, by Leo. H. Grindon.

Q. Is it always painful?

A. No, it is as natural as Birth, and often as painless. It is the falling asleep in rest, and not a sensation.

Q. Ought we to frighten children with the fear of Death?

A. No; it rarely does any good, and often does irreparable mischief. It weakens the moral sense and induces children to do from fear what they would not from the feeling that it is right; and in some cases this dread of death, thus early engendered, embitters the whole of life.

SECTION.

FEELINGS THAT AID IN THE ESTIMATE WE FORM OF OURSELVES, AND INDUCE US TO SEEK THE APPLAUSE OF OTHERS.

SELF-RESPECT, SELF-CONCEIT, PRIDE.

Each person is the centre of his own universe; each carries his World, or at least all that he knows or feels about it, in his own head. We judge of things from a personal point of view, and measure them by the estimate we form of ourselves, and it has been wisely said that whoever makes too little or too much of himself has a false measure for everything—a trifle, plus his ego, is immense; an immensity, minus his ego, is a trifle. Some people's geese are all swans.

Self-esteem is common to all:

> "See some strange comfort every state attend,
> And Pride bestowed on all, a common friend."

It is better perhaps on the whole to have too much of the feeling than too little. Self-confidence within due bounds is very necessary. It is the basis of decision of character. We cannot go straightforward to what we consider right without it; we shall be too apt to be turned by adverse opinion. Of those who have put themselves prominently forward in the world, either for good or for evil, few have been deficient in it. The fear of self-degradation is a powerful aid to the resistance of temptation. Honour, which is in most cases another name for self-esteem, cannot allow its possessor to descend to meanness, to improper pursuits or companions, and it will do much to prevent the debasing indulgence of the inferior propensities.

Richter says, "Do not fear the rise of the sentiment of honour, which is nothing worse than the rough husk of self-esteem, or the expanded cover of the tender wings which elevate above the earth, and its flowers. But to raise and ennoble that honour of the individual into honour of the race, and that again into honour of the worth of mind, never praise him who has gained a prize, but those who rank below him; give the honourable title, not as a distinction for the steps which have been mounted, but as a notification of neighbourhood to what is higher; and lastly, let your praise afford more pleasure because it shows that you are pleased for the distinction it gives."

The object of training is to turn this self-esteem into self-respect based upon truth, uprightness, honour, generosity, and all our highest feelings, and not upon merely external advantages of property, appearance, or accomplishments; and we must take care that the feeling does not degenerate into mere self-importance and pride. Thus, in children we continually see the feeling called into exercise by objects that should never be allowed to excite it; they are noticed for being "nicely dressed," or for their good looks; for their activity and cleverness in some particular way; for being able to recite fluently a number of words with which their memory has been loaded without much thought of their meaning; and for numberless things which have no excellence in themselves, but which produce an abundant crop of conceit.

We have sometimes thought that at a very early age the feeling of self-importance is unduly excited in children even under the most enlightened management. The solicitude which they observe in all around them for their comfort and enjoyment, the watchful care which ever anticipates their wants and wishes, the immediate sympathy which all their feelings receive, conspire to give them ideas of their own importance destined to be cruelly upset when the attractions of infancy are over; if indeed, these ideas do not produce a lasting impression on the character.

If a child has naturally a large share of the disposition under consideration, reproof, unless very judiciously administered, and still more contempt or ridicule, will be apt to increase rather than to subdue it. Instead of inducing humility, they will urge on the feeling to its perversion—self-sufficiency, and create perhaps a moroseness and closeness of temper, which beyond anything else shuts up the mind from happiness and improvement.

When the feeling is in excess, there will be a constant use of "I" and "Myself." Everything will centre in or move round this "I, Myself," and everything will be regarded only as it has reference to this important first person singular.

We have then what Miss Jane Taylor calls "the

loud, loquacious, vulgar egotist." The whole passage is admirable:

"Of those with whom *self* proves the darling theme,
Not all indulge it in a like extreme;
Some have the sense to cover it, no doubt;
Would they had sense enough to root it out!
We therefore bring, as first upon the list,
The loud, loquacious, vulgar egotist;
Whose *I's* and *Me's* are scattered in his talk,
Thick as the pebbles on a gravel walk.
Whate'er the topic be, through thick and thin
Himself is thrust, or squeezed, or sidled in.
Conceiving thus his own importance swells,
He makes himself a part of all he tells;
And still to this he winds the subject round:—
Suppose his friend is married, sick, or drown'd,
He brought about the match, he lets you know;
Told him about Miss B. a year ago;
Or never shall forget, whate'er ensues,
How much he felt when first he heard the news.
A horseman thrown, lay weltering in the mud;
He thought of something that would stop the blood.
A neighbour had a quarrel with his wife;
He never saw such doings in his life!
A fire broke out at midnight in the town;
He started up, threw on his flannel gown,
Seized an old hat full twice as large as his,
And said, *says he*, 'I wonder where it is!'
Was doubtful if 'twere best to stay or go,
And trembled like a leaf, from top to toe.
In vain at times, some modest stander-by,
Catching a pause to make his brief reply,
Cries, 'dear!' or 'only think!' or 'so did I;'
For he, by no such obstacles deterr'd,
Runs on, must tell his tale, and *will* be heard."

In early management it will be better not to notice this egotism—this self-worship and self-exaltation; to be careful not to repeat the child's sayings and doings, and above all things to endeavour to excite an interest *in things themselves for their own sake.* Interest children all day long in their studies, pleasures, and pursuits, and give them no time to think of themselves. Of course we do not mean by this to exclude self-knowledge, of all knowledge the most desirable in such a case. If children are made to feel how all that we possess of real beauty and excellence, whether in body or mind, is the gift of God, without any merit on our part,—how much more of excellence and beauty we might possess had we used due diligence,—how great are our faults and deficiencies compared to that excellence of which we can conceive,—it is almost impossible but that it must engender humility, and prevent them from thinking more highly of themselves than they ought to think.

The feeling may be too weak, and then it leads to irresolution and indecision, to the want of manliness and independence of character, to over-submissiveness and the desire to lean on others. Under these circumstances it must be stimulated.

The abuses of this feeling, in excess, are very numerous. In childhood it gives rise to pettishness and wilfulness, to impatience of control, and rebellion against authority, and to an extreme sensitiveness and readiness to take offence. Later in life it produces pride, arrogance, conceit, love of power, dogmatism, insolence, and tyranny.

Q. Is self-esteem desirable?

A. Yes, it is desirable in the form of self-respect, and to be avoided when it degenerates into self-conceit and pride.

Q. How do we judge other people and things generally?

A. By the estimate we form of ourselves.

Q. Is it desirable to have too much or too little self-esteem?

A. Too much, as it is better that we should over-estimate than under-estimate our powers, and self-confidence is essential to decision of character.

Q. Does not this feeling give rise to the love of power?

A. Yes, and it makes people foolishly think that the highest happiness is to be found in the exercise of authority, in commanding, sitting on a throne surrounded by cringing courtiers, to be worshipped and praised and flattered without reference to desert, but from what is to be got by it. This idea of happiness originates in a savage state, and marks a low phase of civilisation.

LOVE OF APPLAUSE—VANITY.

The love of praise—of the approbation of our fellow-citizens—is one of the strongest feelings we have, and in our present phase of civilisation, as a powerful motive to action, it usurps the place of the love of right. This is strictly to be guarded against in education. Nothing multiplied a hundred times is still nothing: folly multiplied a hundred times is still folly, and a hundred fools do not therefore make one wise man; and yet the applause of the hundred fools is sought more, and is thought to go for much more, than that of one wise man.

This craving for the approbation of our fellow-citizens is not confined to the fools only:

> "Ask you why Wharton broke through every rule?
> 'Twas all for fear the knaves should call him fool."—*Pope.*

It is impossible but that we should wish to stand well in the estimation of others. We must therefore be early taught to value only the sympathy and approbation of the wise and good; and then this feeling, for the present, must have a very limited application.

This craving for admiration is, however, so rarely managed judiciously in childhood, that we seldom see it in mature years subservient to the conscience or love of right. When other feelings have arrived at sufficient strength and maturity, it would be as well to drop the appeal to this altogether. Let the motive be love, or respect, or conscience, or kindness; not praise. Praise, the approval of others, is continually substituted as the incentive to good conduct for those higher motives to which we have before alluded—the satisfaction which results from having done right, and of having assisted to make others happy. "Let Miss Such-an-one hear how well you can say pretty prayers," is a case in point.

It is not intended that praise should not accompany right action, but the wise instructor will make the child understand that the world frequently condemns what is right and approves of what is wrong, and therefore to enable himself to persevere in the path of duty he must learn to feel the consciousness of self-approval or self-respect a sufficient reward.

Richter says, "The desire to please with some good quality which rules only in the visible or external kingdom, is so innocent and right, that the opposite, to be indifferent, or disagreeable, to the eye or ear, would even be wrong. Let a girl try to please with her appearance and her dress, but never with holy sentiments. A so-called fair devotee, who knew that she was so, and therefore knelt, would worship nothing save herself, the devil, and her admirer. Every mother and every friend of the family should keep a careful watch over their own wish to praise—often as dangerous as that to blame—which so easily names and praises an unconscious grace in the expressions of the heart, in the mien, or in the sentiments, and thereby converts it for ever into a conscious one; that is to say, kills it."

To wish to serve and please others is a virtue; to do so for the praise and applause it may beget is to wish to please ourselves, and if not a vice, is nearly allied to one—for we are then satisfied with what begets the praise, and not with the good done. Mere *seeming* will often do this, and it then takes the place of the act and deed itself. Virtue is thus often killed, as Richter says, by becoming self-conscious—by injudicious praise.

In some children, little girls especially, this appetite for admiration is so keen and insatiable that not a word, look, or action escapes untinctured by some covert design upon the admiration of bystanders, and childhood loses entirely its two greatest charms, simplicity and impulsiveness. It is most unfortunate when a mother is unconscious of the strength of this propensity in her child, and deceives herself by mistaking the goodness on the surface for real excellence, and fosters the weakness every minute by indiscriminating praise. Two children may be seen, the one with a great love of praise, the other with little. The latter will sit complacently eating her sweetmeats without offering any to her companions, nothing disturbed by their longing looks and the half-injunctions of the elder bystanders to be a good, generous child, and give some away. The other child, with perhaps an equal love of eating, will eagerly and somewhat ostentatiously share all with her playfellows. The difference in the degree of virtue in the two children is not so great as that one should be reproached as a little selfish glutton, and the other extolled as a pattern of generosity: the difference is simply that the one likes sugar-plums better than praise, and the other likes praise better than sugar-plums. Nevertheless, in nine cases out of ten, the disposition of the latter is very much to be preferred, since the desire for approbation is a much higher feeling than the mere animal pleasure of eating; and a generous action, done even from an imperfect motive, opens the heart, and renders it more fit for the reception of better influences. The greedy child is hardened more and more after every act of greediness, and still more if it is scolded and made to dislike its companions by being placed in odious comparison with them; but a sunshine will be reflected into the breast of the little giver from the happy, grateful faces of the other children, which would be quite sufficient reward, if not overlaid and extinguished by an eulogium.

It is better, therefore, that we should serve or please others for the praise we get for it than not at all, and the feeling is useful. But if it has a wide sphere of usefulness, it is also great in its abuse. It is this love of approbation that is the foundation of all the vices and follies of Fashion. We must do as our neighbours do if we wish for their applause. In savage countries, where clothing is scarce or not much wanted, the inhabitants put rings through their noses and lips as well as their ears, and paint the last fashion on the naked body; or they tattoo themselves, which in the long run is more economical, as then the dress wears for ever, or at least as long as they do. But nothing among savages can at all equal the deformities and monstrosities in the shape of crinolines and head-dresses that fashion of late years has forced upon what are called civilised people. If it is true, however, that the love of dress runs to great excess, we must be careful not to run into the opposite extreme. Beauty of body is desirable as well as excellence of mind, and in checking too great a display of personal vanity we must not inflict upon society an ill-dressed, ungraceful, slatternly "blue," who values only mental superiority, to the entire neglect of the equally legitimate mode of pleasing by the person. Richter says, "While man finds a cothurnus on which to raise and show himself to the world in the judge's seat, literary rank, the professor's chair, or the car of victory, woman has nothing save her outward appearance whereon to raise and display her inner nature; why pull from under her this lowly footstool of Venus? * * We will now pass to the clothes-devil, as the old theologians formerly called the toilet. * * The preachers do not sufficiently bear in mind that to a woman her dress is the third organ of the soul, (the body is the second and the brain the first,) and every upper garment one organ more. * * * Woman's love of dress has, along with cleanliness, which dwells on the very borders between physical nature and morality, a next-door neighbour in purity of heart."

Envy and jealousy spring out of the love of approbation in excess, and it is questionable whether the ordinary modes of school-education do not tend to foster this excess. Zschokke, the great Swiss reformer, says, in his autobiography, "It is treason to the holy nature of childhood to address ourselves in the management of children rather to the covetousness of sordid self-interest, than to the innate consciousness of the true and the noble. The charlatanry of public school examinations was banished from my seminary. They may sometimes prove the merits of the teachers, but never those of the pupils."

Ruskin, from his own experience, also remarks, "How many actual deaths are now annually caused by the strain and anxiety of competitive examination* it would startle us all if we could know; but the mischief done to the best faculties of the brain in all cases, and the miserable confusion and absurdity involved in the system itself, which offers every place, not to the man who is indeed fitted for it, but to the one who, on a given day, chances to have bodily strength enough to stand the cruellest strain, are evils infinite in their consequences, and more lamentable than many deaths."

Childish vanity, another of the signs of this excess of love of praise, should never be treated as a crime; in some instances it might be advisable to let a child learn by experience the paltriness of the enjoyment arising from its gratification. For example, "C. was very vain of some jewels, the gift of an injudicious relative; or, as she emphatically called them, her *do-ills*. Day after day she asked to wear them; day after day her mother said 'No,' but finding that to refuse was of no use, she was puzzled what course to adopt, until it occurred to her to let one fire put another out. Accord-

* Competitive examination for public office is a mistake, as it furnishes no test of *character*. It may keep out the fools, but it lets the knaves through. Certainly no one should be eligible who does not hold certificates of having passed through certain courses of education; but place should depend on character, and not on mere intellectual acumen.

ingly, the next time C. applied to her for permission to wear her *do-ills*, she answered, 'Certainly, wear them if you please; but you know these things are valuable because your Mamma's dear friend gave them to you; they must neither be lost nor spoiled. If you have them on, you must remain in this room, and even I think I should say upon this chair, in order to be sure they are safe.' C. consented to the terms, and joyfully bedecked herself with her finery, and then stationed herself upon a chair. It was a fine evening in August, and the other children were out; however, for two hours C. persevered in sitting on the chair. At length she begged to have them taken off, and from that time to this (two years) the *do-ills* have never been mentioned but with an uncomfortable feeling and a blush. The plan here adopted answered very well to check vanity in that direction; but against vanity about dress and all other things there is but one real remedy, the substitution of love of excellence for the love of excelling; the development of the intellect also will bring about a just appreciation of the value of dress, &c., when weighed against mental superiority."*

Bashfulness arises from an excess of the love of approbation, and modesty is ordinarily connected with little self-esteem; but it has been well observed, "Bashfulness and modesty, although so frequently confounded, have yet no necessary connection or relationship, and either may exist without the presence of the other. The former, or shamefacedness, as it is often called, is a weakness not unfrequently belonging to the physical constitution, and of which every one would gladly be relieved. It may be a quality of those

* "Monthly Repository."

even who are most impure in their feelings, and when unrestrained, most immodest in their conversation. Modesty, on the other hand, pertains especially to the mind, is the subject of education, and the brightest, and I had almost said, the rarest gem that adorns the human character. That awkward diffidence, so frequently met with in the young of both sexes, is of a nature, too often, very little akin to modesty."

However useful the desire of estimation, the love of applause, fame, or glory may be, yet it must be admitted that the feeling from which these legitimate uses spring is far too strong in the present day. How much is done from the fear of the folk, and of what Mrs. Grundy will say, instead of from the fear of doing wrong. Much of what we regard as virtue in the world is merely the tribute which vice pays to virtue—it is merely the *seeming* which this faculty puts on in deference to society, and to gain the name and wages of virtue without its reality; it is not real gold, only counterfeit. This feeling is essentially selfish in its nature, and its characteristic is to love distinction, not the excellence by which alone distinction ought to be acquired; it is satisfied with appearing to be, without being. And herein is the difference between the higher sentiments and this: that these *act*, the other only *talks*; and yet it is very difficult for most people to distinguish between the counterfeit virtue and the real—to distinguish between what is done for applause and out of deference to the opinion of the society in which we live, and what is done from a real sense of rectitude. People are even very apt to deceive *themselves* in this particular. They have all their lives been wearing the clothes of virtue, and talking virtuously, and seeming virtuous, and even doing many virtuous acts; and they wonder at the end of their lives that they are esteemed so lightly. But let such persons examine themselves carefully and honestly, as to whether there has not been more seeming than doing, and whether they have not taken care to get paid in applause for even what they have done. Society, in consequence, instinctively feels that it owes them nothing. They have blown their own trumpet before them—they have let their right hand know what their left has done, and they have had their reward.

That too many work for thanks and gratitude, and not from real benevolence or a sense of duty, is evidenced by the too common saying, "What is the use of helping such people? you get no thanks for your pains;" or "What is the use of attempting to do good? you meet with nothing but ingratitude for your trouble," &c.; whereas, had they been virtuous for virtue's sake—from a sense of duty or benevolence—no thanks or gratitude, which is only praise in another shape, would have been expected. The guinea which is extracted from us in our passage between the plates held by two fashionable or titled ladies,—do we ever think of it afterwards, or watch its application? which we should do, if the good of the cause for which it was given was our object, instead of the payment of a tax to public opinion and the fear of the folk: many subscriptions, and much Church-going, emanate from love of approbation alone.

If we do good to be paid in gratitude, we are certain to be disappointed, and we must learn to do good for its own sake, or not at all. The people generally cannot raise themselves above their own state of feeling, which is one in which the selfish feelings habitually predominate. They judge others by themselves, and can scarcely conceive of a really unselfish motive; or if they can, they would regard an action which has no direct bearing on self-interest as folly. The philanthropist, therefore, must expect to have his motives and actions misjudged and misrepresented. If as a Clergyman he visits the poor, he must hear it said he is only doing his duty; he is paid for it, and he wants to get people to go to Church because he lives by it, the same as another man lives by his shop and is anxious to get customers. If he would serve the poor through the establishment of public institutions, it is considered that power, and place, and social consideration and position are his motives; and the people have some excuse for this mode of viewing things, for they have been too much courted and flattered for the power and influence which their numerical force often confers, and not from any wish to do real good to themselves. We must learn also to do good for its own sake, because the more we study the cause of the evils inherent in society the more we must become convinced that eleemosynary charity, which alone is popular, and paid for in thanks and praise, tends rather to foster and nourish evil than to cure it. To insist upon the only means which are really efficacious to raise the condition of the poor,—providence, prudence forethought, economy, education,—and to help the poor to help themselves, is not the popular course.

There are other minor abuses, such as flattering others, that they may praise us—sacrificing truth and sincerity rather than give offence; but their notice comes more properly under another head. If conscientiousness be naturally strong and well cultivated, there is no fear of the love of praise leading to insincerity and meanness.

But everywhere the spirit of democracy is on the increase, and all men, whether consciously or not, are aiding it by their exertions; and with this increase, and the penny press, and the greatly increasing facility of communication, and, in fact, with everything that enables man to act more directly upon man, public opinion becomes more powerful and irresistible, and in proportion as it thus becomes more powerful is it lowered to the mental and moral level of the increasing multitude from whence that power is derived. No doubt this is good upon the whole, as the world is made for the happiness of all, not of a class; but, nevertheless, it everywhere tends to exalt mediocrity and to make popular that only which is capable of being understood and appreciated, not by the highest minds and intellects, but the lowest. On this account it is that almost above all things moral training must be directed to enable children to act in perfect independence of the public voice, and carefully to study and to do what is right irrespective of it. In America, few have moral courage to breathe a whisper against public opinion; and in France during its late troubles (the wars of 1870-71) not a *single voice* dare speak the truth; and with the increasing power of the majority in this country we are daily approaching a similar condition of mental slavery. We have also equally to guard against the misrule of fashion; for, as George Eliot says, "Our moral sense learns the manners of good society, and smiles when others smile."

The study of the mental faculties, and the legitimate

objects to which they point, will show us that mankind have set up false gods—that they worship golden calves—that the true end and aim of life is sacrificed to these idols, and that if we can but free ourselves from an undue thraldom to custom and habit and fashion, we may be much happier, and attain all that is worth living for, at a much less cost, and at a much less sacrifice. To achieve this emancipation, we must be early taught not to fear the world's dread laugh; but "to stand approved in sight of God, though worlds judge us perverse."

Let children, then, be early taught to set a true and just value on public opinion. Show them how the world has always treated its greatest men—how it stoned its Prophets, crucified its Saviours, martyred its Apostles. Show how fickle, how indiscriminating it is to this day—how ignorance speaks with the same confidence, or even with more, than knowledge—how the heights and depths of the greatest minds are measured at once by the conceit of the smallest. Show how hard it is for people to praise, how easy to blame—how many think they show their sense by being able to find fault, in ignorance that it requires a much higher sense to find out and appreciate excellencies. Call the attention of the young to the kind of criticisms thus current of both men and things in this much-dreaded society, and let them say, if they really seek excellence, whether they ought to value such criticism. It requires great talent and long study to master any one subject; but when they have done so, let them listen to the flippant, trivial, conceited, shallow judgments of the world of their acquaintance upon it, and let them learn from that to appreciate the worth of public opinion, and judge whether the desire of fame, based upon such a public opinion, is worth striving for, or ought much to influence their motives to action. To appreciate a great man requires, if not one as great, still a great man, and the judgments of the world therefore must be either borrowed or erroneous—more frequently the latter, as self-conceit usually supplies any deficiency of talent:

> "Whatever Nature has in worth denied,
> She gives in large recruits of needful pride."

Upon whom does Fame bestow her rewards? Rarely upon those who most deserve them. Does conscience approve the judgment even of the most intimate friends with respect to our own characters; how then can we expect the world, or posterity, to do justice? and praise or blame that is not discriminating and just who would value? The originators of useful reforms are generally persecuted, for they get the ill-will of all who lived on the abuse, while those who are benefited think the good comes from nature. They who really work, and in the modest quiet of their studies gradually prepare the world for new truths, are unnoticed and neglected; but he who becomes the mouthpiece of this public opinion, when formed,—who has brains enough to appreciate, but not to originate, and who can talk,—this is the man whom the world pays, and fame immortalises.

The world scarcely yet recognises any higher motives than those that arise from self-esteem and love of approbation, that is, the love of power and of fame and glory, which is only another name for applause—the stupid staring and the loud huzzas of the multitude. The hero and the silly coquette are still put upon an equality as to motive; both are in pursuit of fame and glory! Power and fame, as means, are perfectly legitimate and worthy objects of desire, but not as ends. As Tennyson says:

> "Fame with man,
> Being but ampler means to serve mankind,
> Should have small rest or pleasure in herself,
> But work as vassal to the larger love,
> That dwarfs the petty love of one to one."

As ends, as something to rest satisfied with, nothing can be more contemptible. The love of power and of applause are perfectly self-regarding, and whatever fine-sounding names they may take, such as love of fame or glory, must be looked upon with great suspicion as motives to action. The trumpet of fame has hitherto been blown before false heroes, and glory has too often waded through blood and slaughter to the world's destruction and desolation. Yet, a young world, making its gods after its own image, could conceive no higher motive with which to invest them. They were made jealous of power, greedy and still more jealous of praise, and their *glory* was regarded as the end and aim of creation. Power was worshipped for its own sake, without reference to the end to which it was applied—even though it was generally recognised as swift to damn, slow to save,—and praise unceasing and indiscriminating was offered up as the most acceptable service and as the best means of turning this power to individual advantage. Gratitude towards a benefactor is a most noble feeling to be fostered and encouraged; but to praise another, whether god or man, for what can be got by it, is of all feelings the meanest. A noise of pots and pans and sounding kettles is used by tribes in Africa to prevent an eclipse, and an equally *senseless* noise of "praise" is used by other tribes to prevent other anticipated disasters, no doubt with the same effect. This abuse of the truly "self-regarding" feelings is most blighting to all our higher aspirations, particularly if it have a religious sanction; and if any portion of such abuse has descended to our own day, the sooner it can be obliterated the better. The abuse of self-esteem is pride; of love of approbation, vanity; and in the present little insight that there is into character, they are often mistaken for each other in their mode of manifestation.

Q. Is the love of praise—of the approbation of our fellow-citizens—a laudable feeling?

A. Yes, when care is taken that the love of applause does not usurp the place of the love of right.

Q. Whose approbation should we seek?

A. That only of the great and good. The praise of the multitude is often of little worth, and in the pursuit of what is right we must accustom ourselves to do without it. Naught multiplied by naught is still nothing, and a hundred fools do not make one wise man.

Q. Are competitive examinations always desirable?

A. No, as they tend to substitute the love of excelling for the love of excellence. Such examinations also furnish no test of character—that is, of goodness and worth—but only of the strength of the intellect. It keeps out the fools, but it may let in the clever knaves.

Q. What too often results from this love of excelling—from this too great love of applause?

A. Envy and jealousy; whereas what we have is none the worse because another has better. Rejoicing in another's good fortune adds to our own happiness; while envy, which is jealousy of another's good fortune, makes us miserable.

PART II.

SOCIAL FEELINGS.

OUR DUTIES TO PARENTS, BROTHERS AND SISTERS, FRIENDS.

THE PARENTAL RELATION.

"Honour thy father and mother" is the commandment, and no doubt this honour includes both love and obedience. But although we may command obedience, we cannot command love. Love is not a voluntary act—that is, we cannot love by willing it: we can love only that which is loveable. The same may be said of honour; we can honour only that which appears to us to be worthy of it. Whether children are able to do their duty to their parents depends therefore very much upon parents themselves—upon their conduct in life and their conduct towards their children. The relationship at present between parents and children is by no means satisfactory. The bonds of discipline have been too much loosened before other ties have been tightened. Mothers are playthings and playfellows, and fathers governors or relieving-officers. Fathers are too much engaged in pushing their position in the world, and mothers have too little education themselves to educate their children and establish a fitting foundation for love and honour to rest on, so that often all that is left for parents is their authority: obedience unwillingly rendered. Parents must recollect that their children were brought into the world without being consulted, and great responsibility rests upon the parent therefore to make them happy when they have been so brought in. They must not come to wish that they had never been born. On the other hand, children must recollect the trouble and anxiety and expense they have occasioned; and that the short term of their parents' life is not long enough to pay what they owe.

The love of parents to their children is too apt to show itself in ridiculous excess; and we must not forget that this over-weening fondness of parents for their own children, as their *own*, is a branch of selfishness, and a powerful check upon the benevolent feelings. A most absurd manifestation of this feeling is the attempt to transfer it to friends and visitors, and the showing-off of children before them. Aided by its strong light, a mother sees a thousand endearing characteristics in her offspring; but such attributes are exactly those which cannot or ought not to be displayed. If it is a little red baby or a very young child that is expected to be admired, then the visitor is the victim; if an older child is expected to show off its pretty ways, its unconscious prettiness or virtue is transformed into a conscious one, and the child is then no longer pretty or virtuous. It is singular that all parents can see this mistake in others, and yet so many practice it themselves, forgetting that philoprogenitiveness, which is the love of our own children, does not necessarily extend in a like degree to other people's. A more serious abuse of the faculty is when the father of a family toils to provide for his children, urges forward their interest in every possible way, spends his health, his life, in securing for them a favourable station in the world, and so thinks all his duties to society fulfilled; when the mother satisfies her conscience in withdrawing from benevolent exertions, in relinquishing her place in the affections of her friends, because—"she has her family to attend to"—neither of them considering that the most valuable part of their children's education should be the witnessing of their efforts for the good of others, for the improvement of society, and the promotion of general happiness. We frequently hear of a person who has thus cut herself off from all her duties to society to attend to her children, that she is a good *mother:* why so is a tigress, in precisely the same sense.

The children follow in the same course as the parents, and so the world makes little progress; nor can it be expected to make much whilst the main object of parents in the education of their children is—not that they may be happy themselves in making others so—but, that "they may get on in the world."

Much has been said and written about spoiling and pampering children, but we are disposed to think that there is more to fear from the opposite extreme of neglect and harshness. The great object in the management of children is to make them happy—to keep them constantly cheerful; to allow no angry passion, no depressing feeling, no fears to take possession of the mind, but to keep the perpetual sunshine of hope and love always bright and clear. This can only be done by constant occupation—not in eating or mere amusement, but in well-selected bodily and mental pursuits. Kindness and gentleness shown towards children beget the like in them. If anger be shown towards or before children, it arouses the same feeling in them. Firmness, not anger, is required in controlling them.

Dr. Combe, in his work on the "Management of Infancy," says, "Let us then not deceive ourselves, but ever bear in mind that what we desire our children to become we must endeavour to be before them. If we wish them to grow up kind, gentle, affectionate, upright, and true, we must habitually exhibit the same qualities as regulating principles in our conduct, because these qualities act as so many stimuli to the respective faculties in the child. If we cannot restrain our passions, but at one time overwhelm the young with kindness, and at another surprise and confound them by our caprice or deceit, we may, with as much reason, expect to gather grapes from thistles or figs from thorns, as to develop moral purity and simplicity of character in them. It is vain to argue that, because the infant intellect is feeble, it cannot detect the inconsistency which we practice. The feelings and reasoning faculties being perfectly distinct from each other, may, and sometimes do, act independently, and the feelings at once condemn, although the judgment may be unable to assign a reason for doing so. Here is another of the many admirable proofs which we meet with in the animal economy of the harmony and beauty which pervade all the works of God, and which render it impossible to pursue a right course without also doing a collateral good, or to pursue a wrong course without producing collateral evil. If the mother, for example, controls her own temper for the sake of her child, and endeavours systematically to seek the guidance of her higher and purer feelings in her general conduct, the good which results is not limited to the consequent improvement of the child. She herself becomes healthier and happier, and every day adds to the pleasure of success. If the mother, on the other hand, gives way to fits of passion, selfishness, caprice, and injustice, the evil is by no means limited to the suffering which she brings upon herself. Her child also suffers both in disposition and happiness; and while the mother receives, in the one case, the love and regard of all who come into communication with her, she rouses, in the other, only their fear or dislike. The remarkable influence of the mother, in modifying the disposition and forming the character of the child, has long been observed; but it has attracted attention chiefly in the instances of intellectual superiority. We have already seen that men of genius are generally descended from, and brought up by, mothers distinguished for high mental endowments. In these cases, the original organisation and mental constitution inherited from the parent are no doubt chiefly influential in the production of the genius. But many facts concur to show that the fostering care of the mother in promoting the development of the understanding, also contributes powerfully to the future excellence of the child; and there is reason to believe that the predominance of the mother's influence upon the constitution of the offspring, in such cases, is partly to be ascribed to the care of the child devolving much more upon her than upon the father during this the earliest and most impressionable period of its existence."

Again, the Rev. C. Anderson, to the same effect, says, "In the laudable anxiety of their hearts, two parents, with a family of infants playing around their feet, are heard to say, 'Oh! what will, what can best educate these dear children?' I reply, Look to yourselves and your circumstances. Your example will educate them; your conversation with your friends; the business they see you transact; the likings and dislikings you express; *these* will educate them; your domestics will educate them; the society you live in will educate them; and whatever be your rank or situation in life, your home, your table, and your behaviour there—*these* will educate them. To withdraw them from the unceasing and potent influence of these things is impossible, except you were to withdraw yourself from them also. Some parents talk of *beginning* the education of their children the moment they are capable of forming an idea. Their education is already begun; the education of circumstances—insensible education, which, like insensible perspiration, is of more constant and powerful effect, and of far more consequence to the habit than that which is direct and apparent. Its education goes on at every instant of time—you can neither stop it nor turn its course. Whatever these, then, have a tendency to make your children, these, in a great degree, *you*, at least, should be persuaded they will be."

Q. What are a child's duties to its parents?

A. Love, honour, and obedience.

Q. And what are a parent's duties to its child?

A. To be worthy of love and honour, otherwise such duties cannot be performed, as we can only love that which is loveable, and honour that which appears to us worthy of honour.

Q. In what way will the interests of children be best promoted?

A. Not by neglecting other duties to make a fortune for them, or by attending solely to them, but by a good example. What we desire our children to become, that we must endeavour to be before them.

Q. Is every mother's darling the finest and nicest child that ever was born?

A. Only to the mother: other people are not always of that opinion.

FRIENDSHIP.

There is no word perhaps more abused in the English language than this. People visit with each other and dine together, and call the circle of acquaintance thus made "seeing their friends." But when adversity comes, and the dinners can be no longer given, and the *friends* fall off, people express their astonishment to find that there was no friendship in the case—merely the gregarious instinct which induces men and other animals to associate and feed together. Friendship, however, is founded upon this instinct, which when strong constitutes what is called "an affectionate disposition," and causes children to nestle in their mother's lap, or sit down and lay their little heads together.

It is a mental attraction of cohesion which causes human beings to cling together and form themselves into compact bodies, acting only upon such individuals as are brought into sufficiently close contact by similarity of constitution and circumstances as to fall within its sphere. Its first and closest bond is family union, the love of brothers and sisters, and all who are in close household companionship, gradually extending to schoolfellows, neighbours, and more distant acquaintance. It is a disposition always seeking to be near its object, mentally as well as corporeally; making the infant restless when removed from its nurse, and the school-girl hurt if her daily correspondent does not tell her every thought of her heart. The habits of the mind are as infectious as those of the body, and the choice of our associates becomes highly influential upon our own disposition. "Tell me a man's companions, and I will tell you what he his."

Children necessarily attach themselves most strongly at first to those who minister most to their comfort and gratification; thus they may attach themselves to those who gratify their pride, or vanity, or appetite; their prodigality or senseless prejudices. When this bond of union is dissolved, and these feelings are no longer indulged, the attachment is alienated.

A great difference is observable in children as to the proportion of this feeling in their constitution. One child seems as if he could not be happy for a moment without his accustomed companions. If he goes to play, they must go too; if he learns, he will do it best when they learn with him. I have known one twin brother commit the same trivial fault for which the other was suffering punishment, that he might share the penalty with him. Another child will pursue his studies and his sports alone, seemingly quite contented and happy without the sympathy of others. Some children, especially boys, will always repel caresses, and for many years wound the heart of mother and friends by an utter indifference to their affection. And yet, if the mind be well constituted in other respects, and the child happily circumstanced, better-founded affection will spring up, and supply the vacuum felt in childhood. A son's love for his mother often grows out of the respect which an insight into her mind and appreciation of her character produce; consequently it is a love deeper in its nature and more capable of growth than this innate, half-animal affection. Hence this love is often far stronger in the man than in the boy.

But this mere feeling of affection is a selfish feeling, fading when the personal benefits upon which it is founded cease. Friendship is something much higher, supported by, if not founded on, all our higher sentiments, and often requiring great personal sacrifices. The first and truest friendship is that which ought to exist between man and wife. If it is not the highest feeling, it is that which makes the largest and sweetest of all returns, for it is beyond all price to have some one with whom you can share everything—all your thoughts, all your feelings, good and bad; upon whom you can lean, upon whom you can rely, who will give life itself for you if required. But the reward is not to be had without the exercise of the duties—for, like charity, friendship "beareth all things, believeth all things, hopeth all things, *endureth all things.*" If it is to be bought, it is to be paid for only in kind. As the poet says:

"Can gold gain friendship? Impudence of hope!
As well mere man an angel might beget.
Love, and love only, is the loan for love.
All like the purchase; *few the price will pay:*
And this makes friends such miracles below."

Q. What is friendship?

A. Not dining out and giving dinners in return, but a deep affection that will induce the sacrifice of ourselves for others.

Q. What is the highest friendship?

A. That which ought to exist between man and wife.

Q. Can friendship be bought?

A. No; "love, and love only, is the loan for love."

PART III.

THE MORAL FEELINGS.

OUR DUTIES TO OUR NEIGHBOUR.

The feelings we have been considering have been called *selfish* because they relate to our own personal or individual well-being. We possess them in common with other animals, and they are the necessary foundation upon which all higher feeling must be based, since it is evident that if we do not take care of ourselves no one could so well take care of us, and neither could we take care for other people. Man does not belong to himself alone, or even to *his own* family or *his own* friends. He is a member of a much larger body—the great body of Humanity. He derives great advantages from this union, as in the struggle for existence opposing circumstances have to contend with humanity, not man. Consequently the duties we owe in return to Society are very great. Society could not exist if they were not performed, and we should have to descend to the level of the brutes—the difference between man and the brutes consisting not only in superior intelligence, but *mainly* in the capacity it gives for this power of combination and co-operation. These duties which we owe to society are called Moral duties, the Science of Morality consisting of the laws and regulations by which we can all live together in the most happy manner possible.

JUSTICE AND TRUTH.

The great principle upon which Society hinges—which indeed alone makes it possible—is Justice. What action and reaction are to the physical world, justice is to the moral. It is useless to disguise the fact under high-sounding words, but justice requires that we should receive, in one form or other, as much as we give. It is thus truly said that we must be just before we are generous, for if we gave all and received nothing our power to be either just or generous would soon come to an end. To insist upon less than the claims of justice is to lower the moral standard—to hold out a premium for improvidence, and an inducement to slackness in the discharge of moral duty. Generosity at the expense of justice is a vice, not a virtue. The world has been acting upon this principle of being generous at the expense of justice, and our eleemosynary charities have everywhere weakened the springs of effort, and lowered and impoverished the population instead of raising it. This spurious charity has created and fostered the disease it was intended to palliate or to cure. To live happily together—that is, in society—we can only exercise our faculties and gratify our own wants consistently with the equal rights of others; and Justice and Right are the same.

The feeling that makes us wish to do what is right is called Conscience. But this feeling by no means tells us on all occasions what is right, and to do therefore what is right we must know what is true. Justice and Truth therefore are inseparable.

The great object, then, of moral education is to strengthen this feeling—this love of Right—and to tell us what is right.

When properly cultivated, the action of this feeling shows itself in a nice sense of justice, straightforward uprightness of conduct, a love of truth, delicacy of manners and sentiments, and that general sincerity and openness of character that peculiarly distinguishes the noblest work of God—an honest man.

Conscience manifests itself very early in some children, and the first little sins which they commit appear to them as great in magnitude as the most outrageous crimes that disturb society, and their feeling of pain in consequence of them is often very intense. A child's conscience tells him that he is much more guilty when he steals a gooseberry out of the garden against positive orders, and eats it hastily for fear of being seen, than when, perhaps in the glee of his heart, he tries his new carpenter's tools upon the mahogany table in the drawing-room. The rebuke, appealing to the reason only for the damage to the table, should be very different to the sorrowing remonstrance or punishment for the theft.

The moral sense is not so early active in many children, and we must especially guard against making matters of conscience of very trifling things. With some parents so many things are wrong, according to the temper they are themselves in, or according to the caprice of the moment, and "naughty" is a word so often repeated, that a child's conscience is without a guide, and becomes completely bewildered. We must be careful not to call a thing wrong at one time and not at another; a child will soon detect our inconsistency. Unless we ourselves have a clear conscience—that is, clear and definite ideas of right and wrong—and unless our principles are consistent, certain, unwavering and undeviating, it is impossible that we can properly guide the conscience of a child. That of which we ourselves have any doubt let us never make a question of conscience with a child. Let us avoid making too many direct appeals to the conscience, for what a child does wrong is not often of much consequence, but when he does wrong knowing it to be so, that is of consequence.

In such a case the sense of guilt should never be suffered to wear away by time in a child's mind, no acknowledgment of it nor reparation having been made. "Never tell a child of a fault without at the same time suggesting some mode of redressing it, which will induce him to put it into practice; for nothing is more to be avoided than that chagrin and discouragement which are the consequence of mere formal correction." * If the sentiment of duty in a child be weak or deficient, it will be the mother's part to lead it on by gentle questioning till the fault committed is brought again clearly before the mind, and being shown in its true colours now that the excitement of passion is passed, it may awaken the consciousness of wrong that was before unfelt.

Nothing tends so completely to weaken the moral sense as undue severity: the pain of having done wrong is often a sufficient punishment. For children of a more advanced age all outward punishment may be

* Fenelon.

positively injurious. When the power of conscience is strong, the feelings deep, and the disposition retiring, often the less notice that is taken of a fault the better. In such a child the sense of demerit will be far stronger, and the repentance more sincere, if he is treated with the same kindness and confidence as before, than if the fault is dragged into public view, and he himself in any degree treated as a criminal; for in that case the wound given to the feelings may be too deep, and good resolves may be turned in a contrary direction.

Justice is the main element of gratitude, the sentiment consisting in the desire to return an equivalent for the benefit received. It may be very early cultivated by requiring from children an uniform courteous acknowledgment of all services received, and a return of kindness by every means in their power.

The world suffers much from *mis-directed* consciences. The office of the feeling, as stated before, is to permit the action of each faculty only so far as is consistent with justice. Right is that which conduces to the greatest utility, and which, *all things considered*, produces most happiness; and wrong is that which produces *unnecessary* pain. But such a rule for calculating what is right, although very well for moralists to establish principles upon, and to decide between the conflicting claims of the morality of different nations and of the customs of society, is evidently beyond the reach of children: they must be taught to have faith in the dictum of their parents. This is right—that is wrong—must be sufficient for them. When an action is to be performed, it will never do to calculate consequences; then all consequences to ourselves and others must be left out of consideration in obedience to calculations previously dispassionately made, and to what we have otherwise been taught to believe is right. The first and the last question must always be, What is right? and it is the principal object of a good education to enable us at once to answer the question; for to doubt, when the feelings are engaged, is too frequently to be lost. Virtue, before it can be depended upon, must become a *habit of doing what is right* at once, and without calculation. If a person is in danger of drowning, it will not do for the person who stands by the water to begin calculating which society can best afford to lose, himself or the one in danger. We have frequent instances of generous individuals who have never even stopped to calculate whether they can swim or not. Not to tell anything but the truth is always right; and in this instance, as in thousands of others equally clear, children should never be allowed to hesitate for a moment, or to think about saving themselves, or saving others, by telling what is false. Truthfulness as a principle is more valuable than the good of any individuals or even nations.

While peace of mind rewards obedience to the dictates of this feeling, the sense of guilt, repentance, and remorse are the pains which punish opposition to them. It is needless, surely, to say that these latter feelings are not virtuous in themselves, and that they are good only in so far as they lead to amendment. The mind should never be permitted to dwell in a sense of demerit, but the feeling of having done wrong should be invariably associated with the endeavour to repair it, and the determination to amend the faulty disposition which induced it. The pains of wounded conscience are only attached to evil for the purpose of its cure.

The feeling which we are considering is the most important of all, because it regulates the proper action of all the others, by confining them within the bounds of what is right—that is, of justice. It makes us desire and love truth and sincerity above all things; and it is painfully evident to all who think upon the subject how much the world needs its proper cultivation. It is disheartening to contemplate the vast area which "Vanity Fair" occupies, in which each acts a part, each wears a mask, each endeavours to deceive his neighbour by passing for something more or less than he is, and each is satisfied with mere seeming, without being or doing. Love of approbation is the prime mover; the craving for *distinction*, not *excellence*—to *appear*, not *to be*. Praise is the grand desideratum, and as *to be* virtuous is often too difficult or too troublesome, the semblance is assumed of whatever will best secure approbation of society. The development of conscientiousness can alone counteract this wide-spreading and infectious tendency. We must strengthen the love of truth, of sincerity, of candour, in our children, and begin early to make them feel heartily ashamed of taking credit which is not strictly their due. Never neglect an opportunity of showing how mean, how dishonest it is.

But how can the love of truth be best implanted, and the dishonesty of society counteracted? First, with reference to speaking the truth. The truth is not merely a literal representation, it is that which does not deceive. In early childhood it is much more easy to teach a child not to deceive than to tell the truth. A child, in trying its new and first acquisition—its faculty of speech—says so much with no other purpose than the pleasure of talking, mixes so much nonsense and pure imagination with the truth, that it is vain to attempt to discriminate between fiction and falsehood, and as useless as vain. We must be very careful, therefore, how we accuse children of falsehood. We must be content to wait till they can themselves discriminate between one and the other, and in the meantime, when their statements are very wide of facts, let us merely say, "Oh, that is nonsense—that is only fun." But as soon as we can—as soon as the proper age will permit—let us train a child on all occasions scrupulously to tell the literal truth, and teach him how to do it. This species of teaching is one of the best exercises the mind can possibly have. Language, although it is too frequently the medium of concealing our thoughts, was not, it may be presumed, given for that purpose; on the contrary, we should always endeavour that our speech should, as near as we can make it, correspond exactly to our thoughts and feelings. How little is this practised; one half of what almost every one says is false—that is, it does not correspond to the real state of thought and feeling, but it is said rather in obedience to the dictates of kindness or politeness, or the desire to please, to show off, and to appear clever. How often is the language of grief upon the tongue with joy sparkling in the eye, and how easy does it seem to compose almost perfect sentences expressive of condolence, of joy, of sorrow, without any feeling whatever in the heart. We must learn to value *truth* above all things, and to do without this inconvertible currency of mere words.

Let the double comparatives and superlatives that now so much disfigure the language of society be discarded, and let us tolerate no exaggeration whatever. Much of what is false arises from the want of not knowing really how to tell the truth, and much from the dishonest wish to make important what we have to tell. Accustom children, therefore, to the strictest accuracy as to when, where, how, and wherefore, and teach them that it is best and most becoming to hold their tongues when an event is not of sufficient importance in itself to be mentioned, and that when it is, the object to be arrived at is not a brilliant relation, but a faithful, clear, and intelligible one. To give a leaning in our speech to the side we wish is almost as bad as direct falsehood, and we should certainly discourage special pleading, and as far as possible teach children to state fairly both sides of the question. Always help a child to tell the truth; for a wilful lie, when detected, must be treated as the most heinous of offences—as the meanest, the vilest, the greatest, the one never to be looked over without punishment.

But we must be as careful not to act a lie as not to tell one. It will be impossible to teach truth and candour to children unless we are truthful and candid ourselves. We must avoid all kinds of double-dealings, double-meanings, reservation; we must never express pleasure at seeing a person, and the reverse behind his back. We must never join in uncharitable opinions of our neighbours. If we are accused we must meet the spirit of the accusation, and not hide behind some little flaw in the indictment; we must not show some little immaterial circumstance to be untrue, and on that account retort upon our accuser as if the whole were false. If we argue, we must not, as is too frequently the case, set up some scarecrow, some dummy of our own, and having shown its unreality, triumph in consequence over our adversary. Above all, we must not *deceive* by telling the truth; this is the worst lie of all—it is betraying with a kiss. We must never promise what we cannot or do not intend to perform, and we must always keep our promise, whether for reward or punishment. We know how difficult it is on all occasions to decide upon the claims of truth, and to judge in what way and how far such claims can be best supported. It is true that much discretion must be used in supporting what we believe to be the truth, and as so much of error mixes with all subjects, allowance must be made for this, and due modesty used in expression; even if we know what is the truth, it is still not to be spoken at all times, but yet on no occasion must we say what is not true or countenance any kind of deception.

But conscientiousness requires honesty as well as truth; dishonesty may be said to be an acted lie. We have got so far in a moral code as an acknowledgment from the world that "honesty is the best policy;" but the world is slow to act even upon this tardy admission, and it generally gives to its honesty a most limited interpretation. Honesty is not merely the not robbing and stealing, but includes Justice—the giving to every man strictly his due. We must not rob others of their time, by want of punctuality in keeping our appointments, or by suffering them to call again and again at our door, when we might have attended to them at once. We must admit every claim that we know to be just, whether in relation to property, character, or intelligence. We must not detract from another's merit, and steal or even withhold his praise. We must give a candid and fair examination to views opposite to our own, before we allow ourselves to speak decidedly upon them. And above all, in measuring out what is due to others, we must never be influenced by what others may do to us, by their opinion of us or their conduct towards us. We are to do as we would be done by, not as we are done by; and if others do wrong it is an additional reason why we should more carefully endeavour to do what is right. In thus regulating our own conduct, we are using the most direct means of cultivating the principle of right in our children. All rules and methods are at best but small adjuncts to the teaching by example, and without that example worse than vain.

It is impossible to say too much against the universal spirit of detraction which so extensively prevails at present that it may be said almost to be the spirit of the age. Rumour is never to be trusted—common rumour is a common liar. No statements, however gross, monstrous, false, and improbable, can be invented against an individual, that are not instantly caught up, circulated, and by the great majority believed without investigation or evidence. That such things should be stated is ordinarily enough to insure almost universal credit, even the judicious and charitable few often presuming without further evidence than "hearsay" that there must be something in such accusations; they cannot be altogether invented; there is never smoke but there's fire, &c. Even those who have been the victims of this lying tendency are as ready and even more ready to fall in with it. It is gratifying to bad people to think that others are as bad as themselves; and in society generally people feel that the easiest way to raise themselves is to pull others down.

There is another untruthful tendency against which we are called upon to be on our guard, equally general, although not equally mean and low in its origin, and which is as prevalent now as it was 2,000 or 3,000 years ago. Mr. Grote, in his history of Greece, says, "Where there is any general body of sentiments pervading men living in society, whether it be religious or political—love, admiration, or antipathy—all incidents tending to illustrate that sentiment are eagerly believed, rapidly circulated, and (as a general rule) easily accredited. If real incidents are not at hand, impressive fiction will be provided to satisfy the demand: the perfect harmony of such fictions with the prevalent feeling stands in the place of certifying testimony, and causes men to hear them, not merely with credence, but even with delight: to call them in question and require proof, is a task which cannot be undertaken without incurring obloquy." Every conscientious person, however, must be thoroughly prepared to meet such obloquy, and he cannot be too sceptical with respect to views and statements thus smoothly and rapidly carried along on the broad current of public opinion. It is astonishing, when once a fact in accordance with public sentiment has been invented, how a thousand apparently confirmatory facts spring up at once, not one of which has the least foundation in truth. The unscrupulousness of the uneducated classes, generally speaking, is almost beyond belief, and is only equalled by their credulity; and both are in proportion to their ignorance. In fact, such is the lying spirit abroad, such the tendency to detract, to exaggerate, and to embellish, that we are not justified in believing anything, to another's prejudice, upon mere "hearsay," and one thing is most certain, that whether we believe such rumours or not, (and sometimes it is out of our power to disbelieve,) we never ought to allow this belief to prejudice the accused as regards our actions without first hearing his side of the question. We shall too often find that the accusation has no foundation whatever, and if it be true, there are frequently extenuating circumstances which will always be taken into account by every just person, who tries to believe the best he possibly can of his neighbours, and wishes to do only as he would be done by.

Q. What are the Moral Feelings?

A. Those which bind men together and enable them to act in unity as well as in an individual capacity. The Science of Morality consists of those laws and regulations by the observance of which we can all live together in the most happy manner possible.

Q. Which are the most important moral virtues?

A. Justice and Truth. We must be just before we are generous.

Q. What is the Conscience?

A. The feeling that makes us wish to do what is right.

Q. Does it on all occasions tell us what is right?

A. No: our Reason only can tell us that. We must know what is true to do what is right.

Q. What is the great object of moral training?

A. To strengthen the love of right, to teach us what is right, and to make the practice of virtue a habit.

Q. How are we to know what is right?

A. We may consult our own conscience, our own friends, and where opinions differ endeavour to ascertain how the best men in all ages have acted under similar circumstances.

Q. Is there any general rule by which right and wrong may be detected?

A. Yes; right is that which conduces to the greatest utility, and which, *all things considered*, produces most happiness. It is that only which, if universally practised, would be for the general good. Wrong is that which gives or leads to *unnecessary* pain.

Q. Can wrong ever be to our interest?

A. No; wrong is always attended by such penalties, mental and bodily, that it may be truly said it never prospers.

Q. Is there any virtue in repentance?

A. It is not a virtue in itself: it is only good when it leads, as it ought to do, to reformation.

Q. What is Truth?

A. That which does not deceive. It is opposed to all double-dealings, double-meanings, reservations, special pleadings, or one-sided statements, and all falseness whatever. A lie is the meanest of all offences. We should never judge without hearing both sides.

Q. What is Honesty?

A. "To be true and just in all our dealings;" to rob no one of their property, time, character, or fame; to give willingly all that belongs to another, without allowing ourselves to be influenced by what others may give, do, or say to us. Honesty is the best policy.

Q. What is the great aim in life?

A. To do our duty. Robertson, of Brighton, truly says that man's real greatness consists not in seeking his own pleasure, or fame, or advancement—"not that every one shall save his own life, or seek his own glory, but that every man shall do his own duty."

VENERATION, REVERENCE, RESPECT, COURTESY.

There is a strong feeling in human nature which induces us to worship, venerate, or respect whatever is considered to be great and good and worthy of respect. This feeling takes a strangely wrong direction in the present day. Men worship the golden calf—that is, wealth; they bow down to rank, titles, ancestry, creeds, customs, laws, and institutions, without reference to their goodness or truth. For almost all other objects of reverence and goodness, we have depreciation, not appreciation.

The aim of education is to give this feeling a right direction, for whatever may be its objects, it is very difficult in after life to break the association between them and the feeling, though reason may plainly point out the absurdity of the connection, and the small inherent claim they may possess to our respect.

The feeling is an important auxiliary in moral training; "it is the chief ingredient in filial piety, and produces that soft and almost holy deference with which a child looks up to its parent, as the author of his days, the protector of his infancy, and the guide of his youth."* It constitutes part of the charm of social intercourse, as the source of the honour we pay to age, to talent, to virtue, and of that courtesy which always distinguishes the truly gentlemanly and polite bearing. Nothing can compensate in this direction for its absence, as we may see in the bold, impudent bearing of some children in whom the feeling is deficient. Although it connects us by a pleasing chain with all that is, or has been, great and good in the moral and material world, in education the feeling has generally been drawn upon too largely, by attaching undue importance to antiquity and authority, considered independently of their real claims to respect. But it must not be undervalued because it has been abused, and if it be deficient in a child it must be cultivated by directing his attention to what is really worthy of his reverence; at the same time showing that we

* Mr. Combe.

also venerate the objects which we would have him honour; for the influence of example is particularly strong over this faculty. Nothing is more chilling to this feeling than derision and ridicule. That which a child hears laughed at by others he can never respect, so that it is necessary most carefully to exclude all such associations from what should be held by him in esteem and reverence. To give the power of appreciation is the great educational work to be done with respect to this great moral feeling, for we have no more right to withhold the respect due to a man than we have to withhold his goods. "He that steals my purse steals trash, but he that steals from me my good name, steals that which not enriches him, but leaves me poor indeed."

And yet the world in general has only at present arrived at depreciation, or the stealing the "good name" and fair fame from all who in any degree possess them. Every fool feels competent to find fault, and thinks that in doing so he raises himself; but it requires a much higher faculty to see the good than to discover defects.

Admiration, Professor Ruskin remarks, is one of the three immaterial things essential to life. "Admiration—the power of discerning and taking delight in what is beautiful in visible Form, and lovely in human Character; and necessarily striving to produce what is beautiful in form, and to become what is lovely in character. * * For Admiration, you (the class to whom the letters are addressed) have learnt contempt and conceit. There is no lovely thing done by man that you care for, or can understand; but you are persuaded you are able to do much fairer things yourselves." And again he says, "A man's happiness consists infinitely more in admiration of the faculties of others than in confidence in his own. That reverent admiration is the perfect human gift in him; all lower animals are happy and noble in the degree they can share it. A dog reverences you, a fly does not; the capacity of partly understanding a creature above him is the dog's nobility. Increase such reverence in human beings, and you increase daily their happiness, peace, and dignity; take it away, and you make them wretched as well as vile. But for fifty years back modern education has devoted itself simply to the teaching of impudence; and then we complain that we can no more manage our mobs! * * * Admiration is the faculty of giving Honour. It is the best word we have for the various feelings of wonder, reverence, awe, and humility, which are needful for all lovely work, and which constitute the habitual temper of all noble and clear-sighted persons, as opposed to the 'impudence' of bare and blind ones." "I believe," says Dr. Arnold, "that *nil admirari* is the devil's favourite text."

Q. What is Veneration?

A. Respect or reverence for whatever we have been taught to look upon as great and good.

Q. To what is it paid now?

A. Too often to rank, title, wealth, without reference to whether their possessors have any title whatever to be considered as great and good; also to creeds, customs, and institutions which are no longer in any way for the good of society; to the dead body of the past whose spirit has long departed.

Q. Which is the higher power, depreciation or appreciation?

A. Appreciation, as it requires that we should possess the virtues ourselves fully to appreciate them in others, and we cannot rejoice too much in the good deeds and noble sayings of others, or in everybody's doing well.

HOPE—CHEERFULNESS.

Among the duties we owe to our neighbour, and more especially to the family circle, is the cultivation of a cheerful disposition. This has not ordinarily been looked upon as a moral duty, but the happiness of all by whom we are surrounded very much depends upon it. The feeling of Hope disposes us to look always on the bright side of things, and it should receive every possible encouragement in education. Hope is the sunshine of the mind, and very much depends on cultivation. There is nothing perhaps in which a greater difference of disposition is observable than in the tendency to look upon the dark or bright side of things.

The first practical lesson which a mother can give to her child on this subject is her own habitual cheerfulness. Long before it can be understood in words it can be felt by sympathy. Her cheerful tone and manner will often dispel the infant's rising tear, and convert it into a smile, and their influence is not less powerful with its growing years. A mother who is sensible of this will never indulge in a discontented, repining tone, whatever may be the vexations she may have to encounter; neither bodily nor mental suffering will lead her into peevishness or fretfulness. She will teach her children by her own example to look on the bright side of everything—to feel, whatever may happen, that

> "The darkest day,
> Live till to-morrow, will have passed away,"

And that thus "though sorrow may endure for a night, joy cometh in the morning." She will show them how to find some good even in what at first appears vexatious and disagreeable, and that what seems to be a misfortune often proves to be quite the reverse. If it be a misfortune, still she will lead them to make the best of it. If they are disappointed of one pleasure, she will point out to them those that are still within reach, and that all is not lost because the desired object is unattainable.

The anticipations of children with regard to future pleasure are apt far to exceed the reality, and we ought to allow for them, and sympathise in them, not making our cool and experienced feelings the measure of theirs, nor expecting them to estimate the value of their anticipated enjoyment by our standard; but if these longings for happiness in store leave the mind restless and disinclined to present duties, they are hurtful and should be checked. A child will soon perceive that pleasure is increased by the consciousness of having omitted nothing for its sake that is right to be done.

If excessive anticipations of good be injurious, the habit of anticipating evil is much worse. This should never be indulged in by young or old. Many of the dreaded evils never come to pass. Let us not throw away present blessings in fears for the future, but let us take every means in our power to avert the threatened ill, and then leave the success of our efforts to wiser disposal than ours. The proper lesson, and one that becomes easier and easier every day it is practised, is that

> "For every evil under the sun
> There's a remedy, or there's none.
> If there is one, try to find it;
> If there is none, never mind it."

Hope is essential to perseverance. If a child, after making one or two ineffectual efforts to accomplish something which he ought to do, or which it is desirable he should do, gives up the attempt despondingly and says, "I am sure I never can do it," we should not only urge upon him the juvenile lesson, "Try Again," but we should assist him to find out the best way of overcoming the difficulty, and even half do the task with him ourselves, rather than allow him to give up. The pleasure of having surmounted one difficulty will stimulate him to the encounter of another.

It is a general idea that there are times and seasons when we ought not to be cheerful, when our feelings ought to assume a saddened hue, and when we should rather encourage the feeling of gloom than endeavour to dissipate it. Perhaps there is truer wisdom in opening as soon as possible the mind, in affliction, to the influence of all alleviating circumstances. A great philosopher and good man used to say that by long habit he had brought his mind to look upon present trouble as he knew it would appear to him afterwards. If we can realise this—if in sorrow we can reckon the comforts we have left, and consider the multitudes who are happy with even less; if we are thankful for what remains, and console ourselves with the reflection that if time cannot replace our loss, yet every day and every hour will tend to reconcile us to it; if we endeavour to enter at once into the state of mind which a week, a month, a year will bring,—then we shall be ready to profit by the lesson of cheerfulness which all Nature joins with the Apostle Paul in giving—"Rejoice always."

Q. What is Hope?

A. The sunshine of the mind; the disposition to look on the bright side of things.

Q. Is it our duty to cultivate a cheerful disposition?

A. Most certainly, as cheerfulness makes life pleasant to ourselves and all around, while grumbling and discontent and a habit of looking on the dark side of things make life miserable. We are what we habitually accustom ourselves to—happiness begets happiness, gladness gladness, ill-temper ill-temper. "If you would not be of an angry temper," says Epictetus, "do not feed the habit. Give it nothing to help its increase. Be quiet at first, and reckon the days on which you have not been angry."

FAITH.

The world, as conceived by us, is created in our own minds by our own mental faculties, and the sense of its reality is the result of Faith. Certain impressions made upon the senses produce within us certain sensations to which we give names as to objects without ourselves, and we believe in their existence as represented by the mind. Mill says truly, however, "that we know nothing of objects, but the sensations we have from them."

The intellectual faculties give ideas, each after its own peculiar mode or form of intelligence; but the *practical belief* attending the action of such faculties is altogether a different thing. The excess of Hope produces immoderate expectations of felicity not founded on reason; and the excess of this feeling of Faith produces credulity. The pleasure and wonder expressed by children and adults who have a considerable development of this feeling, at the relation of marvellous stories, miraculous and improbable fictions, proceed from their extra power of belief—from their giving to such tales a reality in their own minds which to others they do not assume. There is no reason that we can discover why any one cause should produce any one effect more than another, except that it always has done so, and that the end or purpose to be attained requires that it should do so. One thing, therefore, is not more wonderful to young children than another: they believe all things with equal facility. There is equally no real reason why one thing should *not* follow another, however absurd the expectation that it will do so may appear to our mature experience; consequently children believe equally in all things—in the most monstrous prodigies of romance as well as in the most simple and common events—until experience or their teacher has given a proper direction to their faith, and taught them the difference between accidental and invariable antecedence. Neither is this kind of faith peculiar to childhood: almost every one believes in mysteries, and frequently in contradictions, equally with the simplest articles of faith. Children easily believe—they have to be taught to disbelieve. They personify everything, and live in a world of their own creating, which is as real to them as our world is to us. Anything, from a cushion to a boot-jack, makes into a doll, and the doll is a living person—animals talk, trees hold council, and flowers have affections. The extreme eagerness with which children listen to "a tale," particularly if it relates to the wonderful, points out this feeling as a most valuable vehicle for instruction, and for the exercise of our best feelings. While all the faculties of the mind are bent with earnest attention upon the story, they are open to receive the lessons it may convey, and the vivid association of interest will stamp them lastingly upon the memory. No accomplishment is more useful to a mother or teacher than a facility in the power of throwing instruction into the shape of a tale; if this be not naturally possessed, it will become easy by practice. It does not follow that every tale we tell to children must have a moral, and we should be sorry to banish all the old nursery tales which have been the delight of many and many a generation, although entirely unincumbered with any moral, except those that offend against right principle and good taste. The introduction of supernatural horrors to children's minds is, however, greatly to be deprecated.

The proper use of this feeling, and the direction we ought to endeavour to give to it in our children, is faith in ourselves and in those upon whom their guardianship depends: faith whose fruit is confidence and obedience. In childhood all is mystery, doubt, and ignorance; let the child, then, lean upon its parent with that trust which produces hope and love.

Faith is a sentiment, not a mere intellectual perception, and is one of the most powerful feelings we have. It is the foundation of the will, and of decision and energy of character. No one has yet correctly measured the force of will-power based on strong faith.

But if faith is a feeling or sentiment, like all our other feelings, it is blind, and requires equally the guidance of reason in its exercise. It is our faith or belief that guides the conscience, and there has always been a great effort, on one plea or another, to get possession of it; but we are called upon above all things to hold fast to the first great principle of Protestantism—the Right of Private Judgment. Faith must be based upon evidence, and evidence must be furnished by the reason. With those who want to guide our faith it is customary to decry and to vilify poor fallible human reason, but it is all we have for our guidance, and we must not allow ourselves to be deprived of it on any pretext whatever. If we are called upon to submit our reason to revelation, it is reason alone that can tell us what is a revelation, or interpret it when found. It is impossible that any evidence can establish that as revelation which is opposed to reason and the moral sense. Miracle, Inspiration, and Prophesy are supposed to be "the evidences" of revelation; but granting such powers to exist, it is impossible for us to say from whence they are derived, except as we are bound to judge of all other powers—that is, from their tendency.

Veneration, Hope, and Faith are the feelings most exercised by Religion, but the way in which Religion is often taught in early life, both at home and in schools, is very little calculated to call them, particularly Veneration, into legitimate activity. An example may illustrate the home teaching that is but too frequent. "Mrs. — was very anxious (as every right-minded mother must be,) that her child should be religious, and no pains were spared to make him so, as will appear. The boy (not four years old) was brought down to dessert. In due course the nurse came in to take him to bed, when this conversation took place:—Mamma—'Say your prayers, my darling.' Boy—'I won't.' M.—'Oh, yes—now *be* good. Show Miss

Such-an-one how prettily you can say your prayers. (Silent, pouting lips.) M.—'Come now, you don't know what Grandmamma has for you.' Boy—'What?' M.—'An orange.' Grandmamma—'There's Shamrock (the dog,) now, make haste, or we'll get Shamrock to say pretty prayers.' M.—'Yes, dear, now do—because of the orange, you know.' Will it be believed that this chattering had the desired effect upon the boy? Worked upon by greediness and vanity, he lisped the Lord's Prayer in a sulky, muttering manner, was called a good boy, and went to bed, but *without the orange.* When he asked for it, 'to-morrow' was the answer. Here were lessons in plenty: here, in five minutes, were inculcated impressively greediness, stupid surrender of the understanding, vanity, lying, and hypocrisy."* It is sometimes a matter of much difficulty with thoughtful parents how to deal judiciously with the tender germ of religious perception—how to strengthen without injuring by false and unworthy association. Notice the kind of impression which the religious teaching of the nursery often makes upon a child from two to five years old. He talks and asks about God in the midst of his gambols without the slightest reverence, and with a mischievous gusto because it makes nurse look mysterious and shocked; his prayers are a sort of game, till nurse makes them a most irksome task by requiring him to look grave and keep still while he says them. Soon this prankishness may be subdued, and the child may become outwardly decorous, and parents who believe religious education to consist in saying prayers and catechisms, behaving well at church, reading the Bible and being quiet on

* "Monthly Repository."

Sundays, may feel quite satisfied. Meanwhile, if children could give correct utterance to their fancies it would be curious to know the various pictures of God which such teaching forms in their minds. Often the notion is of a colossal human being, sitting on a throne, with his eyes constantly fixed on them. In one child it was an uninviting old man, perpetually employed in making men, women, and children out of dust, and throwing them down to the earth as soon as they were done. In another, it was a great eye, blue and glassy, ever pursuing her; another child used to imagine an eye looking fixedly at her through a crack in the ceiling. It is related of Dr. Doddridge that his mother taught him the Old and New Testaments from the Dutch tiles in the chimney, and accompanied her instructions with such wise and pious reflections as made a lasting impression on his heart. We fear the Dutch-tile association often outlasts the wise reflections.

At our elementary schools every particle of reverence is got rid of. Religion is there associated with lessons and tasks; it is degraded into mere habit and custom and parrot teaching, and a selfish reference to future rewards and punishments, and where a child will "go to" if he does what is wrong. The prevalent scepticism of the working classes is very much owing to this kind of teaching. They lose faith in the rewards and punishments,—the scarecrow set up no longer frightens them, and they have no higher feelings given them.

Indeed, even out of school there is much of the religious teaching of the present day that is subversive of true moral development, and cannot be made to harmonise with our highest powers and aspirations. That the ruling motive should be *our own* everlasting happiness is merely transferring selfishness from this world to the next; and the anxiety for personal safety which is considered to be the proper religious attitude, is opposed to unselfish, disinterested, true nobleness of character. A morbid, sensitive selfishness and solicitude for our own salvation, the fruit of much religious teaching, is in the interest of neither religion nor morality. To seek universal good, in obedience to no commands, and without reference to consequences, here or hereafter, because it is *right*, is the attitude of true nobility of soul. Right is not right *because God commands it*, but He commands it because it is right, and tends to universal good; and religious Faith is trust in God and the immutability of the laws he has ordained for our benefit, and not the stupid surrender of the understanding to illogical and impossible dogmas. Pope's Universal Prayer manifests the proper disinterested religious spirit:

"What conscience dictates to be done,
Or warns me not to do,
This teach me *more* than hell to shun,
That more than heav'n pursue."

Q. What is Faith?

A. The feeling of belief that attends the natural action of all our mental faculties. It is thus natural to believe, unnatural to disbelieve.

Q. Is all belief then equally well founded?

A. No, it is reason alone that can tell us what we ought to believe; and the "Right of private judgment," the first great principle of Protestantism, must therefore always be held sacred.

Q. What are the Religious Feelings?

A. Veneration, Hope, and Faith.

Q. What is the effect of the ordinary teaching of religion in Schools?

A. To weaken faith and utterly to destroy veneration, and as there is also great diversity of opinion and conscientious conviction on this subject, it ought not to be taught in our common schools. Religion is degraded by its association with reading, writing, and arithmetic, and the mere instruments by which we are afterwards to acquire knowledge.

Q. What is Religion?

A. It is the sense of our relationship to God, as morality expresses our relationship to our fellow-man.

Q. What is the highest expression of it?

A. Reverence, awe, trust, and obedience to all God's laws; the resignation of the individual and personal—of all that is selfish—to the Infinite Whole.

Q. Are the Natural Laws, God's Laws?

A. They are merely the expression of His mode of working, and upon our being in harmony with them depends our well-being.

BENEVOLENCE.

"Our being's end and aim" would appear to be happiness; and the object or final cause of the world's existence, the greatest amount possible of enjoyment or pleasurable consciousness. The wisdom of the Creator is evidenced in the design displayed in the universe. Design means the adaptation of means to a particular purpose or end, and we must know what that purpose is before we can say that the means used to carry it out are adapted to the purpose—that is, before we can say that wisdom is displayed in them. If it be denied that the final cause of creation is happiness, we ask what other object can there be? It is said, "the glory of God;" but a world without consciousness, or with a miserable consciousness, would be no glory to God. It is also said the object of creation is "action" and the "development of mind;"

but mere action could as well exist in a world devoid of all spirit or consciousness, and we cannot conceive of any use in increased development of mind, unless it led to increased happiness. If it led to misery, such increased development of mind would be worse than useless, if to indifference it would be the same as a mere increased development of matter.

Thought is said to be "higher far than happiness," but thought that does not lead to the increase of happiness is worse than uselessly employed. The object of thought is to direct and guide all our faculties towards their legitimate gratification, and that legitimate gratification it is that constitutes happiness. It is believed that happiness is allied to pleasure, and that pleasure is only derived from the exercise of the lower or animal propensities; but the shortest and most correct definition of happiness is, that it consists of the sum or aggregate of pleasurable sensation from *whatever* source derived. The happiness derived from the lower feelings is perhaps more intense than that derived from the higher, but it is more fleeting and more mixed with pains. Every joy has its shadow, intense in proportion to its solidity, and such appears to be the necessary law of human nature, that what increases our capacity for joy increases also our capacity for sorrow. There are those who deny that there is any happiness here, and that it is only in the higher pursuits of another world that we can look for it; but in the pursuit of truth, love, and beauty is there no happiness here? and can any one say what is higher? Yes, the path of duty is higher. But is not the path of duty the path of the highest happiness? To a highly-organised human being there is no happiness out of it—only deep sorrow and remorse; and the very pains of the path of duty are joys, so much does the higher nature transcend the lower. A Regulus has infinitely more joy than Nero, although his higher attributes ultimately led to the barrel of spikes. Sorrow and sadness are often only the shortest road to the greatest gladness, and in the regions of faith and hope through which that path leads will be found "the peace of God which passeth all understanding," which is the highest and most enduring happiness of all. Religion is not unsatisfied yearning and aspiration, but action in the path of that duty for which we were created, and trust in God for the final accomplishment of all which our highest yearning and aspiration cannot reach.

Bentham says, "That God willed the happiness of His creatures is indisputable, and he has made it impossible that they should not endeavour to obtain it. To this end He has given them every faculty they possess, and to no other." It is the faculty of Benevolence which places us in harmony with this principal object in creation, and which makes us desire the happiness of others, and gives us a lively sympathy with the enjoyment of all created beings. This feeling has received various names: it is called love of mankind, goodness of heart, good nature, &c., and joined to conscientiousness it constitutes that charity so beautifully described by St. Paul in the thirteenth chapter of Corinthians. As its object is to produce happiness in others, so whenever the feeling is strong in any mind it produces happiness to its possessor, diffusing a genial warmth and sunshine through the mind, which all the frosts and clouds of life cannot dispel; and as it is so powerful a diffuser of happiness, it is most important that we should attend to its early cultivation.

Education, if rightly understood, is that mode of treatment which will teach an individual to feel, to think, and to act so as to produce most happiness to himself and others. This will perhaps be best accomplished by leaving his own happiness out of consideration altogether, and by attending only to duty—to what is just and right. But he must not only *know how*, he must also be *disposed* to act. Now the disposition to act for our own good is already strong enough, as all the propensities tend to that end; but the disposition to act for the good of others depends very much upon the feeling of Benevolence.

As an instinct it is held by some to be possessed, in a degree, by many of the inferior animals. However this may be, its manifestations in man are often simply instinctive. It then forms the character of the good-natured man, who is impelled by it to gratify the wishes of everybody around him, if it be in his power, even at the expense of their future good. He cannot say "No," and he therefore yields to the importunities of the idle and dissolute that which perhaps is due in justice to claims which are, at the moment, out of sight. He spoils his children, gives to their entreaties what he knows to be improper for them, because, "bless their little hearts," he cannot bear to see them cry. If he threatens he cannot find in his heart to perform; if he does punish them, he tries to make amends for it, and to conciliate them by lavishing upon them extraordinary gratifications and luxuries. To diffuse immediate happiness upon those near at hand, without reference to future and more permanent good, is the short-sighted object of the uncultivated feeling of Benevolence.

When cultivated, but with a wrong direction, its operation is still of the same kind, but more mischievous, as it is exerted through a wider sphere. Many of the widespread charities of the present day furnish examples of this. They seek to remedy a present evil, to relieve a present suffering, by means which multiply for the future these pains and sufferings manyfold. A late writer on the principles of Charitable Institutions remarks that they are more numerous—that more exertions are made for the relief of the poor now than at any former period, yet poverty and crime are on the increase. What is the reason of this? The writer alluded to goes on to prove that it is to be found in the fact that remedies are often applied without discriminating between the different causes which produce these evils, and therefore perpetuate and increase them, or at best only palliate them. But the real cause of this want of discrimination and consequent failure is the fact that it is not real benevolence at work, but a something between the *seeming* of love of approbation and a bargain to get as cheaply as possible to heaven. People wish to stand well in the opinion of their neighbours, and they have likewise heard that "he that giveth to the poor lendeth to the Lord," and they approve of the security and invest a small sum, but never more than they can conveniently spare; to do that would be imprudence! They do their charities, that is, give annual guineas, the press generally blowing a trumpet before them; but they neither watch the spending of the money nor care much what becomes of it: consequently, the more remote the sphere of operation—if to build a Chuch at Jerusalem for converted Jews, or to make Christians of Caribs—the more liberal the donation. Children should be early taught to distinguish between seeming and real benevolence—between generosity that costs nothing, that is, involves no self-sacrifice or even self-denial, and that which proceeds from love and duty. When the higher classes are really in earnest about raising the condition of the lower—when they cease to consider them as mere objects to perform their charities upon, as convenient stepping-stones to heaven, as so much raw material out of which they are to work their own salvation, as *the poor* "whom we are always to have with us," and therefore are to be kept poor, or at least in their present position as "lower orders,"—then there will be less difficulty in removing the artificial and ultimately the natural barriers to their success. A little well-directed effort to do good is better than a large and expensive beneficence on a wrong principle.

That which is commonly called charity, the succouring and aiding of distress, is but a limited exercise of benevolence; but that which Paul denominates charity is the true, divine Spirit of Love—"Though I should give all my goods to feed the poor, and have not charity, I am nothing"—that charity which "loveth all things," and which strives to add to the enjoyment of every living creature within its reach.

The desire will grow with its indulgence, until a child will have no idea of happiness except as associated with the happiness of others. Thus, if we wish to create in our child a large heart, extended sympathies, a loving disposition, "identify him," says Richter, "with the life of others, and give him a reverence for life under every form: teach him to consider all animal life as sacred. * * *

"You may teach a higher than Ovid's Art of Love, by requesting your child to do something without commanding or rewarding performance, or punishing neglect; only depict beforehand, if it is for another, or afterwards if for yourself, the pleasure which the little actor's attention to your wish affords. You excite the benevolence of children less by pictures of people's necessities than of the joy produced by relieving them. For the little heart conceals so great a treasure of love, that he is less deficient in willingness to make sacrifices than in the certainty that they would give pleasure. Hence, when children have once begun to make presents they would never cease giving. The parents may give them the reward of certain happiness by a gladly praising approval; an educational lever whose power has not been sufficiently estimated. For children accustomed only to parental bidding and forbidding, are made happy by permission to do some extra service, and by the recognition of their having done it. This affectionate acknowledgment of pleasure renders them neither vain nor empty, but full—not proud, but warm.

"It does the poor man, or dog, or whatever it may be, good, or harm! These few words, said in a proper tone of voice, are worth a whole sermon: and fie! said to a girl, will abundantly fill the place of half a volume of Ehrenberg's Lectures to the female sex.

"Moreover, the author does not attempt to hide from the police, that in the presence of his children he has frequently given to beggars; first, because the appearance of cruelty cannot be removed by any political reasons, nor is it attempted to be; and secondly, because a child's heart, excited by compassion for suffering, should not be chilled.

"Yet a few fragments within the fragment! Do not apprehend too great danger to the affections from children's quarrels. The circumscribed heart of children, their incapacity to place themselves in another's position, and their Adam-like innocence of belief that the whole world is made for them, not they for the world; all these things combine to raise the inflated bubbles which soon break of themselves. They may speak harshly, or even fly into a passion with one another, but must not continue it! You must do many more things to be hated than to be loved by children: hated parents must themselves have hated for a long time. Advancing years rarely awaken a repressed or dormant love; the individual's own selfishness doubles that of others, and this again redoubles that; and so layer upon layer of ice is frozen. You falsify love by commanding its outward expression;—kissing the hand for instance. Such things, unlike kind actions, are not the causes, but only the effects of love. Do not in any instance require love: among grown-up persons would a declaration of affection, if commanded and prescribed by the highest authorities, be well received? It may be again repeated without deserving blame, that the *quickest* alternation between punishment or refusal and previous love is the true, though (to the fair sex) a difficult art of educating the affections. No love is sweeter than that which follows severity; so from the bitter olive is sweet, soft oil expressed.

"And finally, ye parents, teach to love, and you will need no ten commandments; teach to love, and a rich winning life is opened to your child; for man, (if this simile be permitted) resembles Austria, which increases its territory by marriage, but loses its acquisitions by war; teach to love, in this age, which is the winter of time, and which can more easily conquer everything than a heart by a heart; teach to love, so that when your eyes are old, and their sense almost extinguished, you may yet find round your rich couch and dying bed no greedy, covetous looks, but anxious weeping eyes, which strive to warm your freezing life, and lighten the darkness of your last hour by thanks for their first. Teach to love, I repeat; that means—do you love!"*

To love is certainly the highest happiness, and the field for its exercise may be very much widened if we take in, as we ought to do, the whole of the sensitive creation. Here is an unbounded field of sympathy and enjoyment. Each creature has its own world created by its own limited perceptions, and it has also its own field of enjoyment, into which we may all enter with wondering sympathy. Not an inch of this earth—not a remotest corner but is filled with creatures that are adapted to its peculiar circumstances, and are working out the objects of their existence—that is, their enjoyment—in harmony with its conditions. Children should be early taught their duty to animals.† The heart of young humanity is very hard solely for want of cultivation. There is nothing "pays" so well as love and kindness, wherever it may be shown. Others' happiness, including the brute creation, and

* "Levana."

† See Mrs. Bray's "Duty to Animals," (Longmans & Co.,) the object of which is to teach humanity systematically in our common schools.

indeed all our fellow-creatures, however much below us, is always reflected back upon our own, increasing greatly the sum of our enjoyment. Therefore, as Jean Paul says, "Teach to love."

Q. What would appear to be "our being's end and aim?"

A. Happiness—that is, the greatest amount possible of enjoyment or pleasurable consciousness.

Q. What is Happiness?

A. The sum or aggregate of pleasurable sensation.

Q. What is Benevolence?

A. The desire to make others happy.

Q. What often takes its place?

A. The desire for other people's applause, not for their happiness; and it is this false benevolence which originates so much false charity, sapping the very foundations of self-reliance and self-dependence.

THE BEAUTIFUL.

The True, the Good, and the Beautiful form the Moral Trinity. In reality they are inseparable, for the Beautiful is the Holy Spirit—the real essence of the True and the Good. The love of the Beautiful is appreciation, not depreciation; indeed it is utterly opposed to the modern spirit of criticism, which sees only faults—ugliness and deformity.

The sense of Beauty is the highest of all the senses, and based upon the perfection of all the others; in fact, it can only be based upon the full development of all the other faculties. In Art it is too often attempted to be separated from the True and the Good. It requires the most careful cultivation of all the faculties, because in reality it contains all the others. Sir Joshua

Reynolds tells us truly "that a relish for the higher excellences of art is an acquired taste which no man ever possessed without long cultivation and great labour and attention." The feeling begets a love of perfection for its own sake, and due cultivation reveals to us so much beauty here that we do not require to look to any other world for its full gratification.

It has always a refining tendency, and gives an innate shrinking from all that is coarse, low, and vulgar.

The feeling gives not only soul to poetry and romance, but to the prosaic concerns of every-day life, and no station in life necessarily debars us from its pleasures, which, like those of the other senses, ought to be common to all, and be cultivated and improved by all. Wherever there is Nature there is beauty—wherever there is man there should be the faculty to admire. The "privileged classes" have secured to themselves many of the means of its gratification, but they cannot monopolise "the glory in the grass, the sunshine on the flower."

In order to cultivate the faculty, it is not necessary to fill the mind with the false associations and colouring of romance, or to study the models of classical antiquity; but to "go forth into Nature's school," and there it will educate itself, amidst flowers and fields, among the hills, and by the river-side. In towns and cities the lessons of Nature are more faint and few, but even here her sunbeams gild the tops of the spires, and sparkle on the flood which reflects, as it passes by, the crowded habitations; here too the taste may be more readily nurtured upon the beautiful in art and science.

"Children are often very poetical. 'Are you glad that God has made it all so beautiful?' said a child to me as I was watching the sun sinking into the waves at B. The mind of another child of between four and five years old is not less imaginative. During a walk on a fine December day it was delightful to see how happy and observing he was, stopping to look at the mosses, and to gather specimens of the few remaining plants, and talking all the way—'Look at those rainbows on the hills!' cried he, pointing to the different shades of trees, blended in the mists. He gathered a beautiful little piece of moss, and called it his forest; and took up the idea with delight when it was suggested that in that forest all 'the lions and tigers and wolves should play with the lambs, and little children should lead them.'—'And the little baby-boys,' he added, 'should be nursed by elephants, and the lions should put brass upon their claws, for fear of hurting the lambs.' He was told that they could make their paws soft when they liked,—so he carried his jungle full of elephants and tigers carefully home, in his little cold hand. The first mentioned of these children, when four years old, while walking in the wood at ——, wished to gather some flowers for his mamma, who was going away. 'There is no time now,' said some one present, 'but you can send her a nosegay in a few days.' 'They will hang their heads,' said he, 'when mamma goes—they will cry—they will all wither and waste away!' One evening, while watching the sunset, he said, 'The sun sinks behind the deep hills.' When four years old he would amuse himself for hours by drawing lines, and making stories about these lines; for example, 'Here is a steam-boat and here is a little boat, and it goes wave, wave, wave.' But there is no good thing on this earth which may not be perverted, by excess, into bad; his imagination often leads him into untruth. When three years old he said, so very gravely, that had you only looked at his countenance, and not heard his words, you would have felt sure he believed the truth of what he was speaking,—'Do you know, just now I saw a pig walking along the road with a bonnet on.' Every day about this time the habit of telling falsities of this kind grew upon him. Probably he did not wish to deceive; the images passed through his mind, and he wished to communicate them, and knew not yet how to do so but by saying, 'I saw,' 'There was,' and the like forms of expression. However, *had* he meant to cheat, it is a fearful thing to begin with a child upon the subject of untruth, and the plan we pursued from the beginning was not to take the slightest notice of these effusions. To laugh at them would have been fatal, to frown on them scarcely less so; therefore there was no other course left than to remain deaf to them. Tempted on by his imagination, he still tells stories of this kind; but surely these stories are of a very different nature from those which are uttered to screen the teller from punishment."*

If the taste be nurtured upon the beautiful objects and elevated subjects which Nature presents to it, there will be no danger of its becoming sickly and distorted, by being permitted to indulge in the delights of fiction. A pure natural taste will repel all which is incongruous, and assimilate nothing but what is pure and simple in itself.

The love of the Beautiful is a strong guardian of virtue, for they who have tasted its genuine pleasures can never rest satisfied with those of mere sense. But

* "Monthly Repository."

it is possible, however, to cultivate the taste to such a degree as to induce a fastidious refinement, when it becomes the inlet of more pain than pleasure. Nor is the worst of over-refinement the loss of selfish gratification; it is apt to interfere with benevolence, to avoid the sight of inelegant distress, to shrink from the contact of vulgar worth, and to lead us to despise those whose feeling of taste is less delicate and correct than our own. If the beautiful and the useful be incompatible, the beautiful must give way,—as the means of the existence of the many must be provided before the elegancies which can only conduce to the pleasure of the few. Selfishness though refined is still but selfishness, and refinement ought never to interfere with the means of doing good in the world as it at present exists. The beautiful therefore must never be allowed to stand in the way of the more homely virtues, or exercised at the expense of honesty and sincerity.

If the other faculties are well developed and properly cultivated, this will attain sufficient strength of itself. The beautiful is the clothing of the Infinite, and in the contemplation of the beautiful, and the love of perfection, we seek our highest and most intimate communion with the Source of all Beauty, and draw nearer and nearer to Him.

The fine arts—painting, sculpture, music, as well as poetry—ought all to minister to this feeling. The proper use of painting, for instance, ought to be to represent everything that is beautiful in the present, and to recall all that is worthy of remembrance in the past. To give body to spiritual pictures of ideal beauty and perfection—to give a faithful representation of the great and good that have departed, and to put vividly before us those actions and scenes, those pages from universal history which have a tendency to refine, to exalt, and to enlarge the soul,—this is what painting ought to aim at. To paint, however perfectly, horses being shod, deer being hunted, the agony of poor animals in traps, bread and cheese, and lobsters, and foaming ale, is but an abuse, and a perversion of one of the highest gifts and attainments, which a more civilised age will repudiate. A pig-stye, however perfectly painted, still but recalls the idea of a pig-stye; and if it excites any feeling, it is one of regret that such wonderful art should be so misapplied.

Beauty, as exemplified in the person, cannot be separated from the True and the Good, and therefore depends more upon expression than upon feature. As Mr. Smiles, in his admirable work on "Character," observes, even the finest landscape, seen daily, becomes monotonous: so does a beautiful face, unless a beautiful nature shines through it. The beauty of to-day becomes commonplace to-morrow; whereas goodness displayed through the most ordinary features is perennially lovely. Moreover, this kind of beauty improves with age, and time ripens rather than destroys it. After the first year married people rarely think of each other's features, and whether they be classically beautiful or otherwise. But they never fail to be cognisant of each other's temper.

Q. What are the Æsthetic Feelings?

A. Those which give the sense of the Beautiful, which is the highest of all the senses, as it is based on a full appreciation of the Good and the True.

Q. What is its effect upon the character?

A. To give refinement and to elevate the taste.

Q. How may it best be cultivated?

A. By calling attention to the beauty and harmony everywhere around us. The fine arts—painting, sculpture, poetry, and music—are its instruments.

Q. Are the Good and Beautiful always one?

A. The Good, in the present state of the world, is not always Beautiful, but our aim should be to make it so.

Q. What does beauty of person depend upon?

A. Much more upon expression than upon feature.

PART IV.

The feelings of which we have now to treat give concentration, power, and permanence to the others, and may afford equal aid either to our virtues or our vices.

ATTENTION AND HABIT.

We have a feeling which gives the desire to retain present emotions and ideas—an instinctive love of dwelling upon them which helps to form the mind by associating ideas together, and ideas with feelings. Much has been written by mental philosophers upon this power of association, and perhaps the importance of the subject has not been over-rated, as madness is very often induced by the great deficiency of this power, or from its too great excess. But it is not with association we have now to do, but with the power of Attention, which also mainly depends upon this feeling.

The cultivation of this faculty is very important, as little can be done unless the mind can be brought to bear upon the subject before it, and if it can easily be called off and diverted to other things. A concentrated power of attention will often make a little mind go a great way, and take precedence on special subjects over naturally larger minds which are more diffused and without this power of concentration. The judgments of the smaller minds, however, are not always to be trusted out of their special departments of study.

Where there is no original want of this power it is often much weakened by injudicious management in infancy. The active, impatient nurse will not suffer the child's attention to attach itself undisturbed to the object which takes its fancy. No sooner does he grasp the new substance, fix his eyes intently upon it, begin to consider what it is like and what it is for, than she snatches it hastily away, and attracts his notice to something else; thus preventing the little philosopher from making his own experiments and drawing his own deductions. By a constant repetition of this treatment the mind becomes incapacitated for patient and continued thought.

We must remember also that many "children have, in common with weak men, an incapability of instantaneous cessation from what they are doing. Often no threatening can stop their laughter: remember the converse in their crying, in order to treat their weakness as a physician rather than as a judge." *

If, on the contrary, this faculty be constitutionally weak, we must be careful to make the subjects upon which it is exercised as interesting as possible, in order that the pain of giving attention may be outweighed

* Richter.

by the pleasure it will occasion. Let us remember that "there is no memory without attention, and no attention without interest."

Perhaps the excess of this faculty is less common than its absence, but this excess has sometimes to be corrected. It is possible to pay too much attention to a study or pursuit, excellent and important in itself, and to suffer the mind to be engrossed by it to the exclusion of more extended and general information, until we become partial and contracted in our views, and incapable of estimating the true value of our own department of knowledge.

We may sometimes trace the prevalence of the feeling, in a minor degree, in the tenacity with which some persons cling to a subject in conversation, and the pain which they appear to feel when compelled to turn their attention to something else.

When a child seems absorbed so much in one particular mental occupation as to take no interest in anything else, it is desirable that he should be shown how all the branches of knowledge are connected with and throw light upon each other, and how he cannot even know all relating to his favourite subject without enlarging his acquirements.

It occasionally happens that a child appears to be haunted by a particular set of feelings and ideas; they follow him through the day, and form his dreams by night. This, perhaps, is owing to some morbid state of the system, as well as to an excess of this feeling; but in either case the mind should be gently led away to opposite ideas, and both mind and body receive as much relaxation as possible.

HABIT.—Man is the creature of habit; most of his actions are not the result of volition, but of habit, and the great object of the training of the feelings is to produce virtuous habits, for it is habitual virtue only that can be relied upon. Much of the exercise which the mind is required to go through is valuable from no other result but the formation of habit. If nothing else follows from order and system and application, we ought to be satisfied with that. Habits of industry, of attention, of self-subjection, of self-denial, are more valuable than intellectual acquirements, and how we learn is of as much consequence in childhood as what we learn. The continual dropping of water will wear away the hardest stone, and attention and perseverance will overcome the greatest difficulties.

The power of attention mentioned above greatly aids in the formation of habit, and this is of much more importance than has yet been generally recognised. Bodily habits and intellectual habits, with the unconscious or automatic actions based upon them, are well known, but not so the automatic action of the feelings, or their tendency to repeat themselves involuntarily, the mind taking the complexion it is habitually accustomed to, the bright side or the dark side, according as it has been trained. Walking is an acquired habit, so is talking, but these habits are formed so early that we do not observe them. The action of habit in playing on a musical intrument, a piano for instance, is more easily observed. At first each note requires a separate and distinct act of the will, until at last whole airs are played while the performer is thinking and even speaking of something else. This is called the automatic action of the mind, and is the consequence of the mind's acting by or through organisation. We have been long familiar with this action in the department of the intellect, but, as we have said, it has yet to be recognised in the department of the feelings—viz., that the habitual action of the feelings has a tendency to repeat itself involuntarily and without any other cause but its previous action. Even unhappy dreams have a tendency to throw a gloom over the mind in the daytime without our knowing why. Ill-temper begets ill-temper, and becomes intermittent. A happy frame of mind has an increasing tendency to repeat itself, and gladness to beget gladness. On this account it is so important that we should be early trained to look on the bright side of things, for when our future comes into our own hands, the mind may have received its direction and complexion, and our life may be one of habitual contentment, or of grumbling; of the exaggeration of small evils, or the recognition of blessings everywhere. Cultivate therefore above all things a cheerful frame of mind, and the effort, if it requires any, will get easier every day, and eventually will become a habit, and a habit of looking at the bright side of things is a fortune in itself.

Q. What is Attention?

A. The concentration of the powers of the mind upon the object or subject before it.

Q. Is it a valuable quality, and how may it best be cultivated?

A. There is no memory without attention, and no attention without interest. It also greatly aids in the formation of Habit, and our virtues are not always to be relied upon until they become habitual.

Q. What is the most valuable habit we can form?

A. The habit of looking at the bright side of things. As the Spanish proverb says, "If we cannot get what we like, let us like what we can get."

FIRMNESS, PERSEVERANCE, DECISION OF CHARACTER.

Firmness gives strength and efficiency to every virtue and quality of mind. Constancy, fortitude, determination, perseverance, are essential to force of character and consistency in action. The character may be amiable, the wish to do good sincere, but without unity of purpose and perseverance in execution even virtuous efforts will produce small fruits. We have more cause to fear the want of the feeling than its predominance, for what in childhood may show itself in stubbornness and obstinacy, will, if the proper cultivation of all the other feelings be attended to, be displayed in manhood by the virtues of perseverance, fortitude, patience.

With a child who is deficient in firmness, undertakings will be continually begun and continually thrown aside uncompleted in favour of new schemes. Good resolutions, formed when the mind is fresh and active, will give way when the stimulus is withdrawn, or when temptation presents itself.

Where this weakness is observed the force of habit must be brought to bear against it. Regular and constant application must be enforced, and kept up by the assistance of the best feelings, but only for short and certain periods. No disinclination, no idle excuse, must be permitted to postpone the performance of a present duty.

If it happen that the feeling of firmness is stronger than the intellect, it will take the form of obstinacy, because in that case the judgment is not always capable of determining when firmness is misplaced. This frequently occurs, and very delicate management is required to prevent occasional obstinacy from settling down into a habit of perverseness. Some parents and teachers have themselves the love of authority so strong that they would actually prefer that a child should do right because they command it than of his own accord. It requires a stretch of magnanimity of which all are not capable, to be satisfied that their child should judge and act wisely without interference on their part. Their aim seems to be less that of teaching a child to walk alone than to strengthen the leading strings which attach him to themselves. But let them remember that they thus gratify their own propensities at the child's expense. It is a common notion that the first thing to be done in training a child is to "break its will." Are parents sure that this does not arise from the love of power in themselves? Little do they imagine the evils generated in the harsh process!

There are few children who would not obey from motives of affection and duty if they were made to feel that nothing was required of them but what was right and reasonable. Implicit obedience should rarely be enforced, unless the confidence and affection on the part of the child be strong enough to counteract the violence that such a requirement must do to his feelings. Of course this does not refer to very early childhood, when obedience must frequently be required without rendering a reason, plainly because the reasoning power is not developed to receive it; but even then the command itself must be reasonable.

The word obstinacy is often applied to the conduct of children when in reality very different feelings come into play, all producing similar external manifestations. A child may be directed to do something which he thinks involves an injury to himself,—his natural firmness will assist the feeling of opposition in resisting the command; it may include something which he imagines to be wrong,—his firmness will then be supported by his sense of right; or he may not really understand what the injunction means; or may oppose it from the mere superabundance of firmness itself—which last alone is obstinacy, strictly speaking. Now all these cases we are apt to call cases of obstinacy, and treat them in the same manner; whereas they proceed from totally different sources, and require dealing with accordingly. In the last instance we must be sure that the command is *necessary* before it is given, and kindness must unite with determination in exacting obedience. But all occasion for combats of this description should be studiously avoided: it would be almost wiser never to give a command than to give too many. Nothing fosters obstinacy like contention.

Again therefore we say, avoid, if possible, doing battle with obstinacy; to resist the feeling only strengthens it. Employ patience, kindness, reasoning; threats and punishment only increase the evil. Of course there are times and occasions when commands must be given, and when this is the case they must be obeyed *always*, and *under all circumstances;* but such instances should be very rare.

It has been well said, "Firmness is a strong will, obstinacy is a strong won't." The one is an active principle based on reason, the other a mere dead passive one, based on no reason at all.

No eminence is ever reached without continued effort; nothing valuable is ever attained without perseverance: let us, therefore, carefully cultivate a feeling of firmness, which is the base of it. Genius may do much, but it is comparatively useless without that training and culture which steady application alone can give.

Endure hardness, says the preacher—and a large proportion of that which is disagreeable must enter into our every-day life. This feeling will mainly help us to bear it, will put us in harmony with it, and even furnish a kind of pleasure of its own in the fortitude and endurance called for:

> "Into life's goblet freely press
> The leaves that give it bitterness."

To do only that which is pleasant soon engenders a state of mind altogether at variance with steady application and continued effort; it makes self-sacrifice hard and duty difficult. Self-denial must be practised on small as well as on great occasions, and those whose habits are self-indulgent will be weak, irresolute, and easily overcome by temptation.

As a gladiator trained the body, so must we train the mind to self-sacrifice, "to endure all things," to meet and overcome difficulty and danger. We must take the rough and thorny road as well as the smooth and pleasant; and a portion at least of our daily duty must be hard and disagreeable; for the mind cannot be kept strong and healthy in perpetual sunshine only, and the most dangerous of all states is that of constantly recurring pleasure, ease, and prosperity. Most persons will find difficulties and hardships enough without seeking them; let them not repine, but take them as a part of that educational discipline necessary to fit the mind to arrive at its highest good.

Decision of Character.—This is a most valuable

characteristic, and firmness is one of its main ingredients. In action there is nothing like prompt and active decision, and nothing is so painful and stands so much in the way of the highest excellence as the irresolution that often attends even the best people. It is astonishing how the world clears the place for and stands out of the way of a strong Will—of a really resolute and decided person. In the formation of this character much depends upon natural disposition, but still more on careful training. Help a child to decide, and oblige him to stick to it—that is, to be firm. Deciding, which is only another name for Willing, is the last dictate of the understanding, and is often slow in action in proportion to the number of sides of a question a person is enabled to see. Perhaps the best rule that can be laid down to help decision is to consider only what is right and to act upon that, regardless of consequences. We must learn to disregard what people will say, and in the path of duty how it will affect either ourselves or others. Hard as it is to find out on all occasions what is right, still this thinking only of what is right will be found to simplify matters very much. Too much self-confidence, backed by firmness, or rather by obstinacy, which is firmness without reason, is the abuse of this faculty.

Q. What is required to give strength and efficiency to every virtue?

A. Firmness.

Q. What is the difference between Firmness and Obstinacy?

A. Firmness is a strong Will; Obstinacy is a strong Won't.

Q. How is Obstinacy best dealt with in childhood?

A. By contending with it as little as possible.

Q. What is the highest form of Firmness?

A. Fortitude. We require continued effort, but we want a power of endurance, and of self-control also. Hardship is essential to mental discipline, and is necessary to the formation of character and a proper frame of mind.

Q. What is a most valuable mental characteristic?

A. Decision, to which Firmness is a great aid.

Q. How may it best be formed?

A. By confining the mind as much as possible to the consideration of what is right, regardless of what people may say, and other consequences.

IMITATION.

The natural language of every feeling is more or less marked on the person and in the countenance, and no doubt there is a faculty which at once recognises and sympathises with this natural language of the feelings. Through this unknown faculty we gain an instinctive knowledge of character, as through it we enter at once into the mind of another, and for a time may almost be said to become a part of that other mind. From its unusual development in such men as Bacon, Shakespeare, and Scott, is probably owing their deep insight into human nature. As this instinct induces sympathy of feeling, so imitation produces sympathy of action, and copies the manners and gestures of others. Every spirituality or idea, before it can be born into the world, and become manifestable to others, must take some bodily or material form. Imitation copies only that material form, and where the feeling is strong it is sometimes very difficult to distinguish the mere imitation of an idea or feeling from the genuine feeling itself.

Imitation has a very powerful effect in forming and fashioning our minds and habits. It is owing to this feeling, added to the force of sympathy and association already spoken of, that, imperceptibly to ourselves, we take the direction of our feelings and the tone of mind and manners from the age and society to which we belong, and it is not without a strong effort that we can break through the spell which binds us to think, to feel, and to act with all around us. It is intended to make the members of the social body more harmonious. It influences us equally in less important concerns; our gestures, our modes of speech, our habits of life, the regulation of our mutual intercourse, our dress,—all follow the models which the fashion of society sets before us. Owing to this copying propensity, each nation has its peculiar characteristics: the European and the Chinese have each different degrees only of the same mental faculties, but so great is the diversity in their external habits that we might readily believe them to belong to separate planets.

Boerhaave relates "that a schoolmaster near Leyden being squint-eyed, it was found that the children placed under his care soon exhibited a like obliquity of vision."

This faculty seems to be given as the great help in education, but it is a help which throws an immense responsibility upon parents and teachers. The vices and evil habits of parents descend by its means and by hereditary descent from generation to generation; but through the same means none of their excellencies can be wholly lost. Thus a good system of education may do much when aided by a good example, but very little without it. Powerful as is the operation of this feeling, and therefore of example, we must be careful lest children do from the mere imitation of those with whom they associate what ought to proceed from a better feeling—from a higher principle. They who are not in the habit of looking minutely into motives frequently mistake the instinctive action of this feeling for one originating in a higher source. This is a dangerous error, for where imitation alone is the source of good conduct, that good conduct obviously has no root in itself, and will cease as soon as the example is withdrawn. The influence of example, therefore, in order to be a safe, must be a silent one. We must be careful never to say to children, Do so and so because your parents and instructors, those whom you respect and love, do so; but because it is right, it is kind, it is wise. Whilst we gather around children not only circumstances, but persons who will contribute to mould their characters, their manners, and their habits to the standard we approve, we must sparingly, if at all, present them as models; for a child will probably imitate the errors which are associated with the virtues; the mind will also be led to be satisfied with referring to an outward tribunal of right, rather than to the inner one of duty. To place the companions and equals of children before them as examples is more dangerous still, from the risk of exciting envy and jealousy instead of the wish to emulate.

At the same time that we aim at opening the mind to receive all the good which radiates from the examples around, we must infuse into it a principle, which shall enable it to repel the emanations of evil, which are also widely diffused. Singularity is to be avoided if it can be consistently with reason and justice; but when it cannot, then it becomes us to resist the promptings of the feeling which impels us to do as others do—to dare to be singular when the world is wrong; and when we become cognisant of the actual requirements of true humanity in its full development, the amount of time, wealth, and happiness—of the good, true, and beautiful, now sacrificed in the world of fashion—we shall see that it is no small part of the instructor's duty to give this faculty a wise direction, and to check its instinctive manifestation.

There are many obvious abuses against which we shall have to guard in the education of such a propensity. The habit of indiscriminate mimicry tends above all things to the depression of veneration, and, worse than this, imitation is capable of becoming a powerful ally of love of approbation, in seeming to be virtuous instead of really being so.

Q. What is the principal use of Imitation?

A. It makes the members of a family and of society act harmoniously together.

Q. When does it do most mischief?

A. When it induces us to follow a bad example, and when also we do from example what we ought to do from a sense of right. Evil communications corrupt good manners, and we have thus only to know what are a man's habitual companions to know what he is.

THE FEELING OF THE LUDICROUS.

Man has been defined as "a laughing animal," and his dignity need not reject the definition, for it would scarcely compensate him for the loss of the characteristic. When the progress of years and the cares of life have somewhat sobered the spirits, who does not look back with regret to the joyous mirth of his childhood, and if he cannot return to those happy days when he himself was "tickled by a straw," delight in the hearty merriment of those with whom they are not past? One of the happy effects of the mixture of all ages in society is the enlivening influence of the lightheartedness and gaiety of those in whom life is young, upon those whose animal spirits are no longer as buoyant as theirs.

"Laughing is good for digestion," as the old saw hath it, and "he that is of a merry heart hath a continual feast;" but "there is a season for all things under the heaven." In very young children laughter is little more than the expression of a sudden feeling of happiness; in time it becomes, in addition, the outward sign of the sense of the ludicrous, which often shows itself to a degree which demands restraint. They know how to depreciate its effects who have tried time after time to gain a child's serious attention for five minutes, but have failed as often, on account of their pupil's finding at every turn something that excites this feeling. When this happens, the teacher must studiously avoid any word, tone, or look which can awaken a ludicrous association, and pass over without the least notice the child's attempts to break into witticism, until the work requiring attention shall be concluded. Another method was tried with a child whose mirthful mood was quite incompatible with attention to his lesson—he *could not help* laughing, he said. He was advised to jump up, run into a corner of the room, and laugh as hard as he could. He very readily obeyed, and ran laughing to his post, followed by his adviser, who, laughing herself, exhorted him to persevere—"Oh, that is not half long enough; try again." He did his best, but a few minutes were long enough to bring him to his sober senses, and he returned to his lesson quite cured of his risibility.

There may be a strong sense of the ludicrous without the power of exciting it in others, which last is wit, and and depends upon the combination of this sense of incongruity with other mental faculties and peculiarities. In proportion to the degree of intellectual cultivation which accompanies it, will the pleasure it gives be more or less exquisite. Children therefore can seldom enjoy the higher species of wit, because their knowledge is too limited to enable them to understand it; but whenever they can they are quick to appreciate it. They are generally, however, most pleased with humour, drollery, play upon words, and the inferior kinds of wit which depend upon the power of imitation, and their own efforts at wit are for the most part of this class. The sayings of children may be accidentally witty to those who can perceive an incongruity or an unexpected relation which is quite hidden to the children themselves. The laughter thus excited will abash a child of a timid disposition, and add to its natural reserve; while another of a different nature will be emboldened by it to the utterance of fresh conceits, or perhaps to the repetition of the same, over and over again, not doubting that the same effect of surprise and laughter will follow as at the first. When we laugh at such things we should explain to children why we do so, and not leave them with a vague impression on their minds that they have said something wrong, or else very clever. The remarks of an intelligent child of quick perception often contain, unconsciously to himself, the elements of wit. When the child, Charles Lamb, asked his sister in the churchyard, after reading the epitaphs on the tombstones which memorialised the virtues of each of the departed underneath, "And where do the *naughty* people lie?" he did not know that there was wit in the inquiry.

There is so great a charm in the sportive play of fancy and wit that there is no danger of their being neglected and undervalued, or that the native talent for them will remain undeveloped: our chief solicitude must be to keep them, even in their wildest flight, still in subjection to duty and benevolence. We must not allow ourselves to be betrayed into an approving smile at any effusions of wit and humour which are tinctured in the slightest degree by ill-nature. A child will watch the expression of our countenance to see how far he may venture, and if he find that he has the power to amuse us in spite of ourselves, we have no longer any hold over him from respect, and he will go rioting on in his sallies until he is tired, and seek at every future opportunity to renew his triumph. Wit undirected by benevolence generally falls into personal satire—the keenest instrument of unkindness. It is so easy to laugh at the expense of our friends and neighbours—they furnish such ready materials for our wit, that all the moral forces require to be arrayed against the propensity, and its earliest indications checked. We may satirise error, but we must compassionate the erring; and this we must always teach by example to children, not only in what we say of others before them, but in our treatment of themselves. We should never use ridicule towards them, except when it is so evidently good-natured that its spirit cannot be mistaken : the agony which a sensitive child feels on being held up before others as an object of ridicule, even for a trifling error, a mistake, or a peculiarity, is not soon forgotten, nor easily forgiven. When we wish, therefore, to excite contrition for a serious fault, ridicule should never be employed, as the feelings it raises are directly opposed to self-reproach.

The love of the ridiculous often becomes so excessive that the mind is incapable of the effort of being serious for long together, even upon the most serious subjects. It is continually darting off in search of the ludicrous and the absurd, and the associations thus formed are most detrimental to the progress of mental and moral improvement. A peculiar gesture, the disarrangement of a collar or a cravat, the mis-pronunciation of a word, are enough to mar the effect of the most instructive and eloquent discourse. We attempt to reason, and are met by a jest, a pun, a quibble. To turn everything into ridicule is as profitless as it is wearisome. But wit should sparkle amongst the solid endowments of the mind that is fully competent to educate—there should be the power of amusing as well as that of instructing. The influence which a playful wit has over children is shown by the preference which they display at a very early age towards persons who possess it, and the power it exerts not only over them, but over all whose minds are able to appreciate it, proves it to be, when instructed by the intellect, elevated and refined by ideality, and warmed by benevolence, one of the choicest gifts to man which Nature has bestowed.

Q. What is Wit?

A. A sense of incongruity giving a feeling of the ludicrous.

Q. Is it of much value in education?

A. A sense of congruity and incongruity is one of our highest intellectual faculties; it furnishes a valuable test of truth, and enables us to be merry and wise.

Q. What is humour?

A. A mixture of this intellectual faculty with the feelings—the latter predominating. Both Wit and Humour greatly increase with exercise, and in childhood we have not only to guard against their too great activity, but also to give them a harmless and kindly direction.

Phrenology, whether true or not in its organology or craniology, is certainly the most practical system of Mental Science that has yet been given to the world; it is also "the only psychological system that as yet counts any considerable number of adherents." The feelings we have considered are such as by phrenologists are termed *established*, and their connection with nervous centres in the brain is easily discernable by a practised competent observer; and although the list can by no means be considered complete, yet all must admit that it contains the principal elements of our mental nature. Some of the feelings, as they are now delineated in the works of phrenologists, are no doubt too complex in their function, and will be resolved, as the science advances, into more simple elements; but still, as the uses and properties of atmospheric air were the same before it was found to consist of oxygen and nitrogen as after, so any future division or sub-division of the mental faculties will not falsify our present deductions concerning their uses and properties which we have obtained from a consideration of them in the aggregate. It is also beyond a doubt that there are some primitive feelings which are not included in the above list, but enough is not yet known of them to speak decidedly of their education: such are the Love of Knowledge, the Love of the Past, Mental Imitation, &c. As there is a love or desire of property, so also is there a desire for mental acquirement—a love of knowledge for its own sake; and a certain diversity in the mode in which persons mentally connect themselves with the events of life,—some always living in the past, never in the present or future; others never looking back, always forward,—points to some elemental difference for which the faculties we have named are not sufficient to account. So also there is doubtless an intuition into character—a faculty which reads the natural language of the mental states, and which was possessed in a superior degree by such men as Shakespeare, Lord Bacon, and Sir Walter Scott. But incomplete and imperfect as the phrenological classification of the feelings may be, yet, being true as far as it goes, the exposition of the principles of our nature which it furnishes is invaluable in education. To give the use of each faculty, point out the abuse of which it is susceptible, and show in what that abuse consists, must greatly aid a judicious person practically acquainted with the management of children, and in the habit of applying principles to practice. By the assistance of a clever practical phrenologist, or by close attention to natural disposition, the proportion in which each feeling is possessed may be ascertained, and tolerably correct data obtained on which to form our system for the restraint of some feelings and the strengthening of others. It must be admitted that the faculties seldom act alone, but usually in combination with others, and some qualities of mind are of so complex a character that they could not properly be included under any of the separate heads; but still, if each feeling be trained aright, the virtue which is the compound result will be certain to show itself in full strength.

Character and Culture.—Perhaps there are not in any language two more useful educational works—more effectual aids to the formation of Character—than Mr. Samuel Smiles' "Self-Help" and "Character." The latter work, however, with the best possible intention, assumes greatly too much that the mind is a *tabula rasa* upon which any character can be written at pleasure; that we might all be Shakespeares or Newtons if we would but will it and take the necessary steps in training and culture. This is the old mistake, and is still very common, and I mention it because it so frequently leads to the most bitter disappointment. Culture will do a great deal—how much may be seen in the education of the blind and of the deaf and dumb; but no training enables the blind to see, or the deaf and dumb to hear and speak. The mind is connected with organisation, and where that organisation is deficient or defective the mental faculty is so also; and we have intellectual faculties and feelings as blind as the sight without eyes. About one person in eighteen cannot distinguish some colours from others, and one in eighty-nine is colour-blind—that is, cannot distinguish colours at all. All the other faculties, both of intellect and feeling, may be and often are equally deficient, and no amount of cultivation will make up for the deficiency. Of course there are all the degrees between mental blindness and perfect sight, but the most careful training will not make a naturally small power into a large one; and we are only preparing disappointment for ourselves to expect otherwise, as well as too often preventing our making the best of such powers as there are. There is an old and common saying "that you cannot make a silk purse out of a sow's ear," and before you go to work to make your purse it is as well to know the nature of the material at your disposal, and whether you have more than a sow's ear to operate upon. It is as well to recognise the fact, as no truth is valueless, that Character depends more upon Nature—that is, upon the original constitution—than upon training, and although culture may smooth it over and hide it, and produce the *mere seeming* in which we all too much move, it does not materially alter the in-born disposition, which breaks out when conventional restraints are withdrawn and the normal conditions are altered. It takes several generations of careful training materially to alter character and to grow the brain structure upon which it depends.

Q. What is Character dependent upon?

A. Principally upon the original mental and bodily constitution. Culture may do much, but it cannot supply great original deficiency: it may teach a blind man a great deal, but it can never enable him to see. It is the same with all our faculties, both in intellect and feeling, where they are greatly deficient. Our educational efforts, therefore, should be directed by the material we have to work upon.

PART V.

The following subjects could not be properly treated under the same headings as any of the mental faculties taken separately: Authority and Obedience, Temper, Punishment, Manners, Example, Order.

Authority and Obedience.—It is desirable to leave a child as much at liberty as circumstances will conveniently admit, and to give as few commands and prohibitions as possible. Let the child's limbs and affections have full play and free scope, and let our endeavour be to assist the natural growth and enter fully into his mind and spirit. But if a command *must* be given, give it at once as that from which there can be no appeal; the reasons for it are better given afterwards, when there can be no interested motives to prevent the child from seeing them in their proper light. Obedience must always be enforced. The penalty of disobedience must be as certain as the pain which follows the putting the hand in the fire; for a child must be taught what he will find through life—that there is a law controlling his free will for his own good. As much as possible let a child's conduct be the result of his own will, by a judicious arrangement of circumstances about him, rather than of positive command; for what a child may be led to do of himself is much more valuable in its after result than that which is regulated by another's will. There is much in choosing just the right instant for making a demand:

to stop in the midst of any interesting pursuit is always painful. Allow for infirmity of temper, and as much as possible let all feeling subside before commands are given. We may as well command a child not to feel the tooth-ache as not to feel anger and irritation. Never forget what a child must be—that is, what belongs to childhood, and exercise authority as little as possible with regard to those things which a child must necessarily grow out of in a few years. There are many things of which we disapprove which naturally disappear in the course of time. Let not parents, therefore, be too anxious about such things: nature will cure them without their aid.

Q. In what way should Authority be exercised in childhood?

A. In the Family, as in the State, over-legislation is undesirable, and a child should be left as free as possible. Good actions should be spontaneous—not the mere offspring of command. When Obedience is *necessary* it must be exacted *without fail*.

Temper.—Bad temper is oftener the result of unhappy circumstances than of an unhappy organisation; it frequently, however, has a physical cause, and a peevish child often needs dieting more than correcting. Some children are more prone to show temper than others, and sometimes on account of qualities which are valuable in themselves. For instance, a child of active temperament, sensitive feeling, and eager purpose is more likely to meet with constant jars and rubs than a dull passive child, and if he is of an open nature, his inward irritation is immediately shown in bursts of passion. If you repress these ebullitions by scolding and punishment, you only increase the evil by changing passion into sulkiness. A cheerful, good-tempered tone of your own, a sympathy with his trouble, whenever the trouble has arisen from no ill-conduct on his part, are the best antidotes; but it would be better still to prevent beforehand, as much as possible, all sources of annoyance. Never fear spoiling children by making them too happy. Happiness is the atmosphere in which all good affections grow—the wholesome warmth necessary to make the heart-blood circulate healthily and freely; unhappiness the chilling pressure which produces here an inflammation, there an excrescence, and, worst of all, "the mind's green and yellow sickness—ill-temper." Make a child unhappy by continually thwarting him, chiding him, and punishing him, and ten to one he will soon show an evil temper of his own, and a distortion of his moral nature. The friction of trial and disappointment may be very well afterwards, when the character has acquired a degree of elasticity and toughness; but in tender childhood it is purely destructive. The trials of childhood do not prepare for the trials of manhood. That man is stronger to endure and overcome whose childhood has been happy and unruffled. A cheerful temper is the best friend we can set out in life with, and we have a heavy charge to bring against our mothers and nurses if by their petulance and mismanagement they have made us part company. Do not forget what we have already said about the habit of looking upon the bright side of things; that the mind takes the tone it is habitually accustomed to; that ill-temper becomes intermittent. Happiness begets happiness, gladness gladness, and ill-temper ill-temper. The virtues of self-denial and self-control are better fostered under happy than under unhappy influences. Children will delight to make little sacrifices for those they love, if asked to do so in a pleasant tone; and the moral feeling will grow apace under the kindly interchange of good offices between elders and youngers; whereas the dictatorial manner which those in authority sometimes assume immediately gathers the frost about the young heart, and transforms every good feeling into an irresistible desire to be naughty. Bad temper, oftener than we imagine, proceeds from a lurking spirit of revenge for something ugly in our own tone or manner. Fear restrains the child from open resistance or passion; so he takes refuge in sulkiness and a general determination to be disagreeable and perverse. Many persons have a most unfortunate intonation when giving a command, injunction, or reproof—whether to their servants or children—which worse than nullifies all the good they intend. If a mother suspects this defect in herself, we beseech her to ponder over the mischief of letting this association gain strength of herself with the wrong, resistance with the right; and carefully tutor herself till every grain of disagreeable is excluded from her method of reproving. If a mother be positively ill-tempered, the children have but a poor chance; it is next to impossible that they should not catch a malady so infectious; but only those persons who have much to do with children can know how difficult it is to control the temper at all times, and how important. Honour be to the governess who makes the daily tasks pleasant and profitable by her cheerful voice and manner, and overcomes the listlessness or fretfulness of her pupils by a happy mixture of briskness and gentleness; when perhaps, meanwhile, her own poor heart is far away, and burdened with many a sad thought. And also honour to the mother who can bear the noisy overflow of her children's high spirits, when her own are under par, and can return gentle answers to their constant importunate queries, when suffering from bodily weakness or mental anxiety.

Q. How should we treat bad Temper?

A. Generally as a disease, as it is quite as often the result of bodily as of mental derangement. In all cases kindness is the atmosphere in which it is most easily dispelled.

Punishment.—The wholesome administration of punishment demands the most delicate skill and clear-sightedness, with undeviating rectitude of purpose. It is a medicine which, by too frequent use, not only loses all its efficaciousness, but injures and tends to destroy the natural functions of the mind. The mind of a young child in a healthy state—that is, with well-balanced feelings and propensities—is naturally disposed to love goodness and hate wrong-doing, and has a sufficient rectifying power in itself to recover from slight deviations, which is only disturbed and perverted by external interference. If the undue excitement of some selfish inclination has led a child into naughtiness, the aid of the parent may be required by gentle reprimand and the contagion of kindly feeling to restore the balance of moral perception; but this done, no more is needed: the re-awakened conscience will inflict its salutary pain, aided by the humiliation of honest shame. Whenever these best of guardians perform their part, punishment would be only injurious. The love of goodness is restored—only encouragement in the return to it is required. Let the child feel that its parent only wishes him to be good, and let him feel that as soon as he is good he has a right to be happy. As soon as ever the naughtiness subsides, and the desire for goodness returns, there should be no fear of punishment to check it; let the affectionate smile be waiting to greet its first appearance, and no grave lecture recall the sullenness that is past. This winning of children out of their infant foibles is quite different from the weak indulgence which spoils them: clogging their moral stomachs with most deleterious sweets, and destroying their appreciation of healthy food—the bread of life. There cannot be too strict vigilance on the part of parents to keep children from the path of wrong, and to draw them from it by unceasing patient efforts when they have once relapsed. However small the sin—however even *pretty* the naughtiness may appear in its miniature proportions—it is great to the child; its deadly nature is the same, and will infallibly develop itself in time. Let there be no indulgence here—let displeasure attend every fault; but let cordial approbation immediately accompany virtue. So that we should say, as a general rule, let there be *no* punishment—by which we mean the express external infliction of pain, either mentally or bodily—after a fault is over, while the child is yet so young as to be merely under the government of instinct and impulse—that is, perhaps, till the age of five years. There are, indeed, sometimes cases in which a child appears fixed in a state of sullenness or passive rebellion, from causes that are mainly physical, and refuses to obey chiefly from the difficulty of rousing itself out of its sluggish inertness of body; too naughty to take the refreshing run in the garden which would restore its healthy action. It may then be well to rouse the physical energy by a vigorous shake, or even in very stubborn cases by a blow; at all events, this would be much better than serious remonstrance and lecturing when there is no capacity or inclination to listen to it—a beating down of the mind, a moral drubbing, which may give satisfaction to the provoked inflictor, but does irremediable mischief to the bewildered victim. After reason has become so much developed as to be an habitual guiding power, and when transgression has become deliberate, it may be profitable to detain a child more or less in a state of mental suffering, or deprivation of happiness: it may do him good to ponder awhile over his folly and its consequences. He will feel that he has deserved pain; he will acquiesce, or may be led to acquiesce, in his own punishment. Without this acquiescence punishment can never be otherwise than injurious. It will appear merely as a tyrannical power and vengeance, and will stimulate all angry and revengeful feelings in return. As soon as the parent appears in this light of a tyrant his moral power is lost. Rebellion, or, worse still, slavish, cowardly obedience, will ensue. He must be recognised by the child as only the administrator of the Divine law of retribution, which is written upon his own conscience, and then no evil feeling will result—no permanent evil feeling, even though the human infirmity of the parent should lead him to undue severity.

There is, however, much misapprehension as to this

Divine law of retribution and what has been called responsibility for our actions. Responsibility merely means that we must in all cases bear the natural consequences of our actions; it does not mean retribution or revenge, or vengeance for actions which, being past, cannot now be prevented. If actions are wrong they are attended by pain, physical or moral, which pain is intended to show that they are wrong, and to prevent their recurrence in future. All punishment is, and ought to be, reformatory in its character. Nature's punishments are sharp in proportion to the necessity for her immediate interference. If a child approaches too near the fire it is burnt, and the pain is sharp and immediate; if it were not, probably the child would be destroyed. We should imitate nature's modes of punishment, and as much as possible let the punishment be the actual consequence of wrong action. "A burnt child dreads the fire," and few injunctions are required to keep a child out of it. This is the way nature teaches the difference between good and evil, and if she punishes it is always for good.

Q. What is Punishment?

A. The penalty of ill-doing.

Q. Ought it to be directed to the past or the future?

A. It should never be retributive, or directed to the *past*, as that cannot now be avoided; but always to the future, as that only is in our power. All punishment, therefore, should be reformatory in its character, its object being to correct offences and to prevent their repetition. All other punishment is revenge: it is cruel and wrong.

Q. Are punishments required in early childhood?

A. Very seldom, and when they are they should be short and sharp.

MANNERS.—Few persons in these days are so cynical as to maintain that manners are of no consequence. Though they are but the external surface of character, and therefore not of the vital importance which belongs to the inner heart and root of it, still it would be absurd to deny that the qualities of that surface do very much concern the happiness both of the individual and of society. If beauty alone were in question, (but in fact beauty is closely allied with moral health,) the outward grace of manner would deserve and repay such sedulous care. The gardener's labour is not spent in vain when he cherishes into bloom merely the brilliant-tinted flower. The wise cultivator of the human plant, however, will bear in mind the analogy of nature, and will not think he can produce that beauty by painting the surface. If art can add a tint to the flower it must be by laying no pigment on the petal, but by infusing a new chemical element into the soil, which must ascend through the pores of the stem, and be elaborated in its secret glands. And so to cultivate manners that will be really attractive we must labour from the heart and soul of man outwards, and they in their turn will re-act upon the heart, and aid the growth and development of virtuous character: as those flowers and leaves with their polished surfaces imbibing the sun and air give back nourishment to root and stem.

Good manners should be cultivated because, first, they *are* good: they are beautiful, suitable, proper; they gratify the artistic perception in ourselves; a refined mind would prompt to elegant action in a solitary wilderness;—in the second place, because they are agreeable to others, and to give pleasure is no mean branch of benevolence. Let the best motives be present to the mind of the teachers and the taught, and the work will be incomparably best performed. Let children be trained to sit quietly, to talk gently, to eat with nicety, to salute gracefully, to help another before themselves, because it is *proper*, it is kind, it is becoming to do so; not because Mrs. Grundy will stare at them and think them naughty if they do otherwise. It is best of all to behave prettily because it *is* pretty; it is well to behave prettily because it will please Mrs. Grundy; the lowest motive, which leads to merely artificial and counterfeit elegance, is to behave prettily because Mrs. Grundy will think it pretty.

Politeness, which Johnson describes to be "the never giving any preference to oneself," frequently, we know, lies all upon the surface. Still this is better than the absence of it; for, as we have already intimated, the habitual regard to observances which are prescribed upon the principles of benevolence, which is at the root of all politeness and good manners, will lead by degrees to the love and practice of benevolence itself. And when it is considered how contagious are all the feelings of our nature, whether good or evil—how the frown will excite an answering frown, as smiles will kindle smiles—how the rude jest will provoke the insolent reply—how he who always takes care of number one will find himself jostled by a host of equally independent units, whose bristles are roused in emulation of his own—it is evident that the well-being of society is affected in no slight degree by the regard which is paid to the outward decencies and amenities of life. Manners *(mores)* may not now mean morals, but they are the best possible substitute.

Manners ought to be merely the outward and visible

sign of the inward and spiritual grace. Each faculty, or inward grace, has its natural language, or outward sign, in the person; and if the inward feeling begets the outward expression, so, in a minor degree, will the outward expression beget the inward feeling. Hence the great importance of Manners. That which was mere seeming at first, put on in deference to mere conventional usage, in time becomes the real thing itself—the virtue of which it was the mere outward form.

Q. What are good Manners?

A. The outward expression of our best feelings.

Q. Why should we be polite?

A. Because the outward expression of good feelings begets the same feelings in others; because grace and refinement add beauty to life, and politeness furnishes the oil which enables society to work without friction.

Example.—We must here again repeat the great rule in education—Be yourself what you wish your children to be; or to express it more practically—Be yourself under the guidance of the same principles as those by which you would guide your children. There may be natural reasons why a parent cannot in all things be a pattern for his children. Besides difference in age, there may be infirmities and deficiencies over which he has no control; besides which, they may be differently constituted, so that the rule which is right for him may not be applicable to them. In the striving, then, after excellence, rather than in any condition of Being actually attained, he must be an example to his children, and never, through any false idea of maintaining his authority, inspiring reverence—in short, humouring his own pride, attempt to concentrate their view on himself as their beau ideal, and so heap a weight of responsibility on his own head which he is naturally incapable of sustaining.

The duty, then, of parents and teachers in the matter of Example is twofold: to make right principles living realities by their own obedience to them, and to gain such an attractive power over the minds of their children that they too shall be brought into the same subservience.

It does not necessarily follow that children imitate their parents or instructors; they will invariably imitate those who most forcibly fix their attention. A mother or governess may be most wise, most virtuous, most everything; but if there happen to be in the nursery or neighbourhood any who will amuse their fancy with marvellous stories, answer all their questions, and invent fascinating games, these geniuses will be, in the child's judgment, authorities of a much higher order than the keepers of the law in the parlour. Superiority of mind in itself, and the tendency to quietness and reflection which the possession of knowledge gives, often add much to the indisposition of grown-up persons to amuse children in their own way; and a romping nursemaid will therefore soon obtain a hold over them which the mother fails to do. Whoever can make children the happiest will have the most influence over them, and it is much easier to make them happy by exciting their animal spirits than by interesting them mentally. Persons of coarse, uneducated minds generally appeal directly to these animal feelings in their efforts to amuse children, and will draw away affection and influence from the careful instructors who try to make way by delicate and less exciting means. Parents, then, must learn the art of inspiring interest in the pursuits which they themselves direct, and there must be such happy associations with all the intercourse between them and their children, that no gratifications which can be procured from other sources shall really have a counteracting charm.

It is piteous sometimes to see what a dull place the drawing-room is made to a child, and how it must soon learn to hate the society of its parents and their friends. So long as it sits quietly and makes no noise, and looks like a little block of wood, it is called a good child, and perhaps overwhelmed with kisses,—that is to say, commended for being inanimate and indolent, and for making no use of its faculties. But as soon as it begins to grow restless, to pull about everything within reach, and to urge eagerly, and perhaps noisily, oft-repeated questions concerning the nature and reason of this thing and that;—the bell is rung, the child is considered a nuisance and given to the servant, and while its little heart is bursting with shame and disappointment, which it can only express by cries and sobs—"naughty child" is reiterated, and it is again banished to the nursery. It is in fact punished for being happy—for employing its powers—for making its own best efforts for expanding its little mind; and precisely at the moment when the faculties are in the best possible state for receiving right impressions they are checked, bad feelings are excited, and it is sent amongst those who may perhaps misunderstand its wishes, and thwart or punish its anxious desire to *know;* leaving the poor child with a deep and bitter sense of unjust treatment.

It is granted that children must not talk and be

troublesome in company; and one use of a nursery is to prevent this. There they may have full play to work off the animal effervescence in active games and bodily exercise of all sorts, and the quieter amusements should be reserved for the parlour. A supply of little occupations, adapted to his capacity, and made interesting by the explanation and occasional participation of his elders, are the best preventives to the restlessness which makes a child troublesome. And whenever a child can amuse himself without interfering with the comfort of others, it seems a pity that he should be kept to the nursery. The little creature is always imbibing sideways, so to speak, a portion of all he sees and hears, and his character is fed every instant by the atmosphere of habits and ideas around him. Can we, then, be too cautious with whom we place the child in contact? Surely not; and yet must we not say that, in ordinary cases, nursemaids, grossly ignorant, are the chief companions of the young in early childhood? Easy, indolent mothers think themselves fortunate when they have a nursemaid who amuses the children well, and keeps them happy all the day long without any trouble to herself: it is so much burden off her shoulders. She is a little annoyed certainly to discover that they have caught the nurse's grammar and accent, and perhaps sets herself to work to correct this with much vigilance. She does not consider that when she has succeeded in laying a fine coat of varnish on the surface, the tone of thought and feeling which has been imbibed deeper down lies entirely untouched. In fact, in proportion as the children are made happy out of her sight, she must be careful to watch over their moral growth, because, as was said before, a child's heart opens immediately to receive impressions from any one who makes him happy.

But if it be granted that our nursemaids are inefficient, do we find that mothers, even among the higher classes, are usually adequate to their office? If we look but to the education, the training, which young ladies commonly receive,—to their course of life at that period of existence when they ought to be qualifying themselves for the important trust which may hereafter devolve upon them,—the question answers itself. What part of their studies or pursuits bears any direct relation to the responsibility they take upon themselves? They come to the task, ignorant of the anatomy, the physiology, the mental constitution of the young being who belongs to them, and of all the most important provisions for insuring its health and happiness. Engaged in the frivolous pursuits of the world, introduced into society at an early age, dressing, dancing, visiting, ritualising—when they are called to the most momentous duties, they are obliged to rely upon an ignorant nurse, to trust to old women's tales, for what ought to have been correct knowledge. It is a fortunate circumstance in this case if the mother has sense enough to know her own unfitness, and to delegate the office to some one who is qualified; but if she has true reason to believe that she possesses the gift of making children happy, and of guiding and governing them well at the same time, it ought only to be strict necessity that prevents her being their chief and almost constant companion. Those children are much privileged who believe their mother to be a treasure of all excellence, as well as their own best friend, and if she can gain, by fair means, such a compliment as a little girl of three years old paid her mamma, "You are the bestest and beautifullest of all," she will rejoice at it, and turn the conviction to good account, whatever hallucination there may be in the matter.

Teaching by bad example we believe to be a fatal error. It is often maintained that young people—that is, boys or young men—should be made acquainted with the world and its wickedness, in order that they may avoid it: as the Spartans exposed their drunken Helots to teach sobriety. This is a very dangerous experiment. Custom and example have always a tendency to become stronger than morality and principle. Under strong temptation, the mere knowledge that a thing has been done, or is done, weakens resistance, and the first step in vice is thus made more easy. After the first step the road presents few obstacles. Keep the mind pure and in ignorance of the ways and wickedness of the world in early life at least, until the principles are fixed and the vision clear enough to see distinctly where the road leads to.

Q. How are children best taught?

A. By example—by endeavouring, as much as possible, to be what we wish them to be. Our actions have always much greater force than our words.

Q. Is it right to teach by bad example?

A. Teaching children by principle what they ought to do, and by example what they ought not, is the wrong method. The mind should be kept pure, and as far as possible in ignorance of the wickedness of the world, until the character and principles are formed. Then only is it safe to teach by bad example.

ORDER AND METHOD.—Nothing is more important in education than teaching orderly habits. There should be a place for everything, and everything in its place. There should be a time for everything, and as much as possible everything should be done at that time. All things by repetition become easy—by repetition at stated times they become easier; in this way they become habits, and learn to perform themselves even without our aid. The health of both body and mind much depend upon the assistance Nature receives in this respect. By punctuality we must endeavour to join ourselves on and to become part of the "order of nature." By order, method, and punctuality only can we economise our time, occupy every minute, and accomplish any great work. Unoccupied time leads to desultory habits both of thinking and acting, of all things to be avoided. Order and method, and organisation, are the same things. The Post Office is the best example we have at present of what order or organisation can effect. We may put a letter now into a hole in the wall almost everywhere, and the answer to it will be brought to our own door almost immediately, and a penny each way pays the cost and leaves a considerable profit. The world at present, comparatively, is a complete Chaos, but we have only to follow this example of the Post Office, and introduce Order, and all may then receive those external advantages of civilisation which hitherto have been confined to a favoured few.

Q. What is Order?

A. Having a place for everything, and keeping everything in its place. Having a time for everything and doing everything at that time. It is the great economiser of all work, and alone will secure the leisure which we all require, and to which we all ought to be entitled.

PART VI.

THE EDUCATION OF THE INTELLECTUAL FACULTIES.

The education of the Intellectual Faculties is no part of the object of the present work; still, "as we must learn what is true in order to do what is right," and as it is the special function of the Intellect to teach us what is true, I shall make a few remarks upon the subject.

The mode in which Intellectual Education is at present conducted calls for the remark that we must be careful not to lose the end of the cultivation of the Intellect in the means we take to acquire it. Thus, as Mr. Combe says, we must have "an early conviction that man is made for action; that he is placed in a theatre of agents, which he must direct, or to which he must accommodate his conduct; that everything in the world is regulated by laws instituted by the Creator; that all objects that exist, animate and inanimate, have received definite qualities and constitutions, and that good arises from their proper, and evil from their improper application." These are the proper objects or ends of knowledge, and it must always be borne in mind that reading, writing, arithmetic, languages, and mathematics, disconnected from their application to realities, though highly useful in exercising the mental faculties and in preparing the mind to receive knowledge, are not *knowledge*, but the mere instruments of acquiring it, and it is only in such a light that they should be regarded. If a boy's time and attention be engrossed by the acquisition of these mere instruments of learning, as the case has hitherto too much stood, it is a chance that he may lose all taste for the knowledge which they are to fit him for acquiring. Let him be introduced into the kingdom of nature itself, and he will imbibe a taste for and love of knowledge, which will always remain with him, and which will make him eager to acquire the means of obtaining it.

The mind having become acquainted with the existences around, their properties, their relations,—being stored with the facts of natural history and science—having observed the motions that are going on, physical, chemical, and vital—it will begin to inquire into their causes, and the reflective powers will come into more especial operation. The study of science may now be entered upon, the knowledge acquired arranged under its proper heads, and each fact placed in the department to which it belongs. A clear and concise arrangement for this purpose has been given by Dr. Arnott in the "Table of Science" contained in the Introduction to his Physics. It is of great consequence that both teachers and pupils should carry in their minds a clear conception of the general field of human knowledge, and of the comparative importance of its several sub-divisions; and perhaps, as he affirms, this is the most valuable single acquirement that the mind can make. It is because I am so decidedly of this opinion that I have introduced any allusion to the Intellect in this work. The field of literature gets larger and larger, and young minds start without any chart for their guidance through the weary waste. It is most important to all further attainments that we should first possess ourselves of the simple fundamental principles in all the great departments of science. It must have been observed that the confidence and dogmatism with which opinions are ordinarily advanced are in proportion to a person's ignorance; but perhaps it is not too much to assert that no one is really in a position to give an opinion upon scarcely any subject who is ignorant of such first principles. Dr. Arnott's table enables us to get a clear view of where these are to be found; we shall therefore give it here, with the substance of the valuable remarks attached to it:

"TABLE OF SCIENCE.

1. PHYSICS.	2. CHEMISTRY.
Mechanics,	Simple substances,
Hydrostatics,	Mineralogy,
Hydraulics,	Geology,
Pneumatics,	Pharmacy,
Acoustics,	Brewing,
Heat,	Dyeing,
Optics,	Tanning.
Electricity,	&c.
Astronomy,	
&c.	

3. LIFE.	4. MIND.
Vegetable Physiology,	*Intellect,*
Botany,	Reasoning,
Horticulture,	Logic,
Agriculture,	Language,
&c.	Education,
	&c.
	Motives to action.
Animal Physiology,	Emotions and Passions,
Zoology,	Justice,
Anatomy,	Morals,
Pathology,	Government,
Medicine,	Political Economy,
&c.	&c.
	Natural Theology.

5. SCIENCE OF QUANTITY.

Arithmetic,
Algebra,
Geometry,
&c."

"Supposing *description of particulars*, or *Natural History*, to be studied along with the different parts of the *System of Science* sketched in the table, there will be included in the scheme the whole knowledge of the universe which man can acquire by the exercise of his own powers; that is to say, which he can acquire independently of a supernatural *Revelation*. And on this knowledge all his arts are founded,—some of them on the single part of Physics, as that of the machinist, architect, mariner, carpenter, &c.; some on Chemistry (which includes Physics), as that of the miner, glass-maker, dyer, brewer, &c.; and some on Physiology (which includes much of Physics and Chemistry), as that of the scientific gardener or botanist, agriculturist, zoologist, &c. The business of teachers of all kinds, and of governors, advocates, linguists, &c., &c., respects chiefly the science of mind. The art of medicine requires in its professor a comprehensive knowledge of all the departments.

"As the sciences are all intimately connected with each other, great advantage must result from studying them in the order above given,—for *Chemistry* cannot be well understood without a previous knowledge of *Physics*; and *Life*, consisting of Animal and Vegetable Physiology, is a superstructure on the other two, and cannot be studied independently of them. This method of proceeding, therefore, will prevent repetitions and anticipations, and considerably diminish the labour of acquirement.

"It thus appears that the *Science of Nature* may be considered as a continuous and closely connected system of history, which to be clearly understood must be studied according to the natural order of its parts, just as any common history must be read in the natural order of its paragraphs. But so little has this been known, or at least acted upon, in general, that perhaps no other human plans formed with one object have been so dissimilar and inconsistent as the common plans of education.

"The notions on education prevalent in the world until recently have been as erroneous with respect to the comparative importance of different branches of knowledge as with respect to the order of study. Thus at many of our famed Schools, and even Universities, the attention has been directed almost exclusively either to *Languages* and *Logic*, or to *Abstract Mathematics*; the preceptors seeming to forget that these objects have no value but in their application to Physics, Chemistry, Life, and Mind. The reason for bestowing much attention on the Greek and Roman languages was good some centuries ago, because then no book of value existed which was not written in one of these languages; but now the case is completely reversed, for he who learns almost any matter of science from old books is learning error, or, at the least, knowledge far short of modern erudition. As to the higher mathematics, again, while they merit great honour, as being the instrument by which many useful discoveries have been made, and the conjectures of powerful minds have been confirmed, still a very deep investigation of them is neither possible to the generality of men, nor if it were so would it be of utility. The mode of proceeding, then, to which we have alluded, is just as if a man, to whom permission were given to enter and use a magnificent garden, on condition of his procuring a key to open the gate, and certain measures to estimate the riches contained within, should waste his whole life on the road in polishing one key, and procuring others of different materials and workmanship, or in preparing a multiplicity of unnecessary measures. This and many similar errors arise from persons not being in general taught to carry in their minds a clear conception of the general field of human knowledge, and so of the comparative importance of the different sub-divisions,—the possession of which conception is perhaps the most valuable single acquirement which the mind can make. He whose view is bounded by the limits of one or two small departments, will probably have very false ideas even of them, but he certainly will of other parts, and of the whole; so as to be constantly exposed to commit errors hurtful to himself or to others. His mind, compared to the well-ordered mind of a properly educated man, is what the misshapen body of a mechanic, crippled by his trade, is to the body of the active mountaineer, or other specimen of perfect human nature.

"We now proceed to remark, that by arranging science according to its natural relations, and therefore so as to avoid repetitions and anticipations, a very complete system might be exhibited in small bulk, viz., in five volumes, of which the separate titles would be, 1st, *Physics;* 2nd, *Chemistry;* 3rd, *Organic Life,* or *Physiology;* 4th, *Mind;* and 5th, *Measures* or *Mathematics.* From such works, with less trouble than it now costs to obtain familiarity with one new language, a man might obtain a general acquaintance with science. And such is the close relation of the departments of science with each other, that consummate skill in any one may generally be acquired more easily, by first studying the whole in a general way, and then applying particularly to that one, than by fixing the attention from the beginning upon the one more exclusively. The study of Anatomy thus becomes very easy to him who has first studied Physics.

"Were such elementary treatises once in existence, they might be maintained complete by a periodical incorporation of new discoveries; and if furnished with correct and copious references, they might form an index to the whole existing mass of knowledge. This *Book of Nature* would be of more value to the world than any other conceivable institution for education, for it would convert the minds of millions into intellectual organs of advancement; while in the crowd, many would probably be found in every age, as highly endowed by nature as any that have appeared along the extended stream of time."

It is scarcely possible that an individual thus introduced to the world and to himself should not acquire a taste for knowledge and a thirst for information. The principles of science are now so much simplified, that they may be made comprehensible even to ordinary understandings, and neither sex should be excluded from the intellectual tastes and enjoyments to which such knowledge must lead.

The *Science of Physics*, or *Natural Philosophy*, explains the causes of the phenomena of the material world, and furnishes never-failing subjects of interesting inquiry;—all the ordinary occupations of life, all that is going on in the world of nature, are, in fact, series of experiments in Natural Philosophy, which may be explained and made interesting to children at a very early age. The reasoning powers may be thus directed to all the changes that are going on around, the causes of most of which are easy of explanation, and may be illustrated without difficulty by simple experiments. Sir David Brewster says, "Philosophy in sport never fails to become 'Science in earnest:' the toy which amuses the boy will instruct the sage; and many an eminent discoverer and inventor can trace the pursuits which immortalise him to some experiment or instrument which amused him at school. The soap-bubble, kite, balloon, water-wheel, sun-dial, burning glass, and magnet, have all been valuable incentives to the study of science."

Chemistry shows us how all the different kinds of matter go to form the endless variety of substances on the face of the earth.

Life introduces us to the animal and vegetable kingdoms, with their different divisions and classifications. It explains the principles of vegetation, and gives to the garden, to the flowery mead, and to every hedge and bank a ten-fold interest. It introduces us to the wonderful structure of our own frames, to that of animals, and their comparative anatomy, to the laws of health, to all the phenomena of sensation, self-motion, growth, decay, death, &c., and to all that we as yet know of their causes.

The Science of Quantity, or *Mathematics*, gives us rules for applying the measures or standards that express quantity, and for comparing all kinds of quantities with each other.

The study of *Mind*, the most important of all, introduces us to ourselves; it makes known to us our feelings and intellectual faculties,—their character and nature,—the end they are intended to answer, *i.e.*, their use, and it also explains their abuse,—it shows their proper and legitimate sphere of action, and the relation they bear to things and circumstances—and ultimately, how they may all be used so as to insure to their possessor the largest return of happiness of which his nature is capable. This knowledge is simple, as we have endeavoured to show in the foregoing part of this work, and may early be brought home to the mind of a child; he may be made to understand the nature of his faculties,—he may be led to see clearly the distinction between the selfish feelings and those that tend to the happiness of others, and thus learn to analyse the motives of his actions, and become ashamed of such as are purely selfish. No kind of knowledge can be so calculated to prevent the abuse of the faculties, and to assist the teacher in moral training, as such a knowledge of self.

This is a sketch of the education which the Intellectual Faculties must receive, if we would exercise them all, and upon their proper objects. In this manner the nature and properties of all things around—their relation to ourselves and happiness—will be learned, and in a manner that cannot fail of being pleasurable rather than painful and compulsory. Dr. Arnott beautifully observes with reference to the department of Physics "The greatest sum of knowledge acquired with the least trouble, is perhaps that which comes with the study of the few simple truths of Physics. To the man who understands these, very many phenomena, which to the uninformed appear prodigies, are only beautiful illustrations of his fundamental knowledge,—and this he carries about with him, not as an oppressive weight, but as a charm supporting the weight of other knowledge, and enabling him to add to his valuable store every new fact of importance which may offer itself. With such a principle of arrangment, his information, instead of resembling loose stones or rubbish thrown together in confusion, becomes as a noble edifice, of correct proportions and firm contexture, and is acquiring greater strength and consistence with the experience of every succeeding day. It has been a common prejudice, that persons thus instructed in general laws had their attention too much divided, and could know nothing perfectly. But the very reverse is true; for general knowledge renders all particular knowledge more clear and precise. The ignorant may be said to have charged his hundred hooks of knowledge, to use a rude simile, with single objects; while the informed man makes each support a long chain, to which thousands of kindred and useful things are attached. The laws of Philosophy may be compared to keys which give admission to the most delightful gardens that fancy can picture; or to a magic power, which unveils the face of the universe, and discloses endless charms of which ignorance never dreams. The informed man, in the world, may be said to be always surrounded by what is known and friendly to him, while the ignorant man is as one in a land of strangers and enemies. A man reading a thousand volumes of ordinary books as agreeable pastime will receive only vague impressions; but he who studies the methodised *Book of Nature* converts the great universe into a simple and sublime history, which tells of God, and may worthily occupy his attention to the end of his days."

It is the especial characteristic of the British nation to prefer practice to what they call theory, by which they mean principles. They know where the shoe pinches, and wait till it does pinch, and then have their last made accordingly, without any absurd reference, as they would consider it, to either anatomy or physiology. This leads to as many different opinions as there are experiences in life. In Mathematics, having first agreed as to our fundamental principles, we are all pretty much of the same opinion; and the same may be said in a somewhat less degree with respect to the Physical Sciences; but in all that relates to Mental Science—to Man's Nature and Development, there are scarcely two opinions alike. There are no generally recognised fundamental principles, and the diversity of opinion is most striking. The shoe, however, is beginning to pinch in this direction, and we are beginning to think that something more should be done in Education, although we are far from being agreed as to what that should be. Thus Dr. Neil Arnott, in the appendix to his admirable "Observations on National Education," says, "On the occasion of the great International Exhibition of the products of industry, held at Paris in 1867, the remark was made by intelligent judges that great progress had been made in civilised countries generally since the first International Exhibition at London in 1851, the result being due no doubt to the very useful lessons then given to all interested visitors. But it was further remarked that the advance had been more considerable in several other countries than in England; for that, whereas England had previously stood highest in the markets of the world in regard to quality and cheapness of products, there were now other countries nobly rivalling her in important articles. The cause of this change, in the opinion of competent judges, was that the technical education of the industrial classes has been more improved in other countries than in England, in regard particularly to the natural sciences of natural philosophy and chemistry, shown by Lord Bacon and others to lie at the foundation of the sciences and arts.. It was remarked that in the primary and other schools in Britain the subjects mentioned were scarcely taught at all; and that in the higher schools and universities the chief honours and prizes and profitable appointments in the public services were given, not for proficiency in the studies which fit people for useful activity among their brethren, but for familiarity with the literature of the two dead languages, Greek and Latin; in which languages books are no longer written, while the books that have come down to us were composed by men who knew nothing of the momentous discoveries in science and the arts which are the main groundwork of our modern civilisation.

"The facts here referred to have caused mortification to many in this country; and a strong desire has been felt to remedy the faulty state of things. Already important steps have been taken with this view. A loud demand has arisen to enforce the studies of the natural sciences. In the universities new professors have been added. In the public schools of Eton, Westminster, &c., teachers are now appointed, and motives are offered to attract to the study of science by rewards assigned to proficiency. And further, an enlightened foresight has led private individuals to give important aid, as in the case of Mr. Whitworth, the distinguished engineer, who, having accumulated wealth while greatly benefiting the public by the exercise of his scientific skill, has founded thirty annual scholarships of 100*l.* each, to be gained by students in the natural sciences. Again, Mr. Peabody, a native of the United States of America, of English extraction, had for a long time been distributing with admirable judgment hundreds of thousands of pounds, in various ways, under the influence of his opinion 'that education is a debt due from present to future generations.'"

Dr. Arnott tells us that he also has hoped to promote the study of the natural sciences as part of public education, by establishing in several of our universities scholarships for meritorious students.

A deputation, also, of the Council of the British Association for the Advancement of Science, consisting of the president, the general secretaries, and the treasurer, Sir Charles Lyell, Bart.; Sir John Lubbock, Bart., M.P.; Dr. Lyon Playfair, M.P.; and Mr. Francis Galton, had an interview some time since with the Vice-President of the Council, when they presented the following document:

"SIR,—The deputation from the Council of the British Association for the Advancement of Science waits upon you for the purpose of urging the advisableness of including elementary natural science among the subjects for which payments are to be made under the authority of the Revised Code. We have asked you to receive us at the present time because we understand that you have announced your intention of making certain modifications in the code. Our reasons for requesting you to give direct encouragement to the teaching of natural science in elementary schools are three. Firstly, we conceive such teaching to be one of the best instruments of education in the sense of intellectual discipline, and in many respects better calculated to awaken intellectual activity than other studies; secondly, we think that a knowledge of the elements of natural science has a high value as information; and, thirdly, we are of opinion that scientific training and teaching in the elementary schools will afford the best possible preparation for that technical education of the working classes which has become indispensably necessary to the industrial progress of the country.

"We take the liberty of pointing out to you that, in asking for the introduction of scientific teaching into the elementary schools, we are not seeking for the creation of a new system or even of new executive machinery. The Science and Art Department does already provide for elementary scientific instruction; and all that is necessary to fulfil our desire is, that the system of the Science and Art Department and that of the revised code shall be brought into harmonious co-operation. In preferring the request that instruction in the elements of science shall be made part of the regular course of instruction of all elementary schools, we desire carefully to guard against the supposition that we are seeking for such an amount of this kind of instruction as would interfere with the teaching of reading, writing, and arithmetic, and the other essential constituents of primary education. On the contrary, we think it very desirable that systematic instruction in elementary science should be given only to those scholars who are able to read and write fairly; that it should be limited to certain well-defined subjects, such for example as elementary physical geography; elementary physics and chemistry; elementary botany; and, in consequence of its relation to the public health, elementary human physiology; and that care should be taken to make the instruction, so far as may be, real and practical.

"Finally, we desire to point out that such scientific instruction in the elementary schools as we pray for would afford a means by which any child of exceptional aptitude for scientific pursuits might obtain the education suited to its capacity in the higher schools, and that in this way advantages similar to those which are offered by the scholarships and exhibitions of grammar schools to the children of the well-to-do classes of society would be extended to the poor and necessitous. In other countries in which well organised systems of secondary education for the working classes exist, it has been found necessary to give a taste for science in the elementary schools, so that the youth of the country may be induced to take advantage of the more advanced schools. While, therefore, we look with pleasure to the introduction of science into the endowed schools of the country we still believe that it will be necessary to link them to the elementary schools by commencing instruction in science in the latter."

The address was signed by Professor Huxley, as president of the British Association.

CONCLUSION.

Morality simply means the Laws under which, or the Rules and Regulations by which, men may live together in the most happy manner possible. Man's great power consists in combination and co-operation; and civilisation increases as the latter gains strength: as a bundle of sticks he is strong, as a single stick he is weak and easily broken. The great moral maxim, therefore, is, help one another—live for others as well as for ourselves. The moral laws are thus known to us by observation and experience quite as much as the physical laws.

On this great round world on which we all find ourselves we could not even live unless we helped one another; or, as Ruskin puts it, "It is the law of Fate that we shall live, in part, by our own efforts, but in greater part, by the help of others." And hence the Moral and Social Laws.

A child can easily and early be made to understand the nature of this bond of union between the members of our race.

Thus: Suppose a little infant were left to take care of itself as soon as it was born. For how long would it keep alive? It depends upon some one else to feed it and clothe it and cherish it; and the mother saves it from perishing because she loves it as if it were part of herself.

Suppose again that children had to provide for themselves. How could they do it? They might be healthy and strong, but how could they build themselves a house to shelter them, or make clothes to keep them worm, or find food to eat, unless some, older and wiser than themselves, found all these things for them? The father provides for his children, and gives them a home and food and clothes. He loves them as part of himself.

But the father could not provide for his children unless others helped him to do it. He must have people about him who will build his house, grow his food, make his clothing, in return for what he gives them or does for them.

And so it is of the whole family of mankind.

They must all work for one another, in order to live.

They must be just and truthful to one another, in order to live peacefully.

They must love one another, in order to live happily. And therefore the great commandment is "Thou shalt love thy neighbour as thyself." And if this is not always possible in the present state of the world, as we can only love that which is loveable, and all are not loveable, still we can the more sedulously perform the duties of love, and strictly do what is just and right.

In the development of the moral character we must by no means lose sight of the connection of the mind with organisation. Education may be defined as the developing and perfecting of all the faculties which make a complete man. All these faculties are connected with the brain, and the first requisite therefore is a large and healthy and well-formed brain. To insure this it is essential that it should be placed in conditions for its healthy growth. We cannot engraft virtue on physical misery. People must be happy themselves to make others happy. We must live in an atmosphere of happiness and justice to stimulate the brain to activity in that direction. With increased exercise comes increase of growth, and that increased growth is transmitted to offspring. To grow the organisations upon which moral action habitually depends is the work of time, and we must be content to wait.

Another essential point to be observed in relation to the connection of mind with organisation is that the brain developes itself in a given order; certain parts arriving at maturity before others. The selfish or animal feelings and the perceptive faculties come first to maturity,—next the moral feelings,—and last of all the reasoning powers are developed. We should in consequence be very careful not to over-work any part of the brain or mental faculty which is but imperfectly developed. Great and serious mischief has arisen, and is constantly arising, from the neglect of this law, and from ignorance of the gradual steps by which our faculties are unfolded. It should be our effort therefore to assist and not to force their growth by giving them more exercise than their immature state will bear.

Dr. Caldwell, in his valuable little work on Physical Education, observes, "Parents are often too anxious that their children should have a knowledge of the alphabet, of spelling, reading, geography, and other branches of school learning at a very early age. This is worse than tempting them to walk too early, because the organ likely to be injured by it is much more important than the muscles and bones of the lower extremities. It may do irreparable mischief to the brain. That viscus is yet too immature and feeble to sustain fatigue. Until from the sixth to the eighth year of life, the seventh being perhaps the proper medium, all its energies are necessary for its own healthy development, and of that of the other portions of the system. Nor ought they to be directed, by *serious study*, to any other purpose. True—exercise is as essential to the health and vigour of the brain, at that time of life, as at any other; but it should be the *general and pleasurable exercise of observation and action*. It ought not to be the compulsory exercise of tasks. Early prodigies of mind rarely attain mature distinction. The reason is plain; their brains are injured by premature toil, and their general health impaired. From an unwise attempt to convert at once their flowery spring into a luxuriant summer, that summer too often never arrives. The blossom withers ere the fruit is formed."

Parents, then, must be satisfied to wait for the effects of the best-regulated system of training until all the faculties are matured. If a child of early age be selfish, it is not a sufficient reason for its continuance in selfishness after the period when the moral feelings, owing to greater physical advancement, act with greater strength;—neither if a child be dull and stupid, intellectually considered, is it necessary that he should remain so after the period when the reasoning powers are fully developed. We cannot look for the full fruits of judicious mental cultivation until after fifteen or sixteen years of age, when all the feelings and mental faculties will generally have attained their natural growth and strength.

An important result of the union of the mind with organisation is the influence of the passions—of each feeling or group of feelings—upon the health of the body, and upon the duration of life, as well as upon our habitual cheerfulness and happiness. It is the characteristic of the propensities or selfish feelings never to be satisfied; and as to produce the same excitement the drunkard is obliged each day to increase the dram, so all our propensities—Ambition, Love of Power, Love of Acquisition, &c.—crave increased excitement to produce the same pleasure; until at last, with advanced age, such sources of enjoyment fail, and they who have trusted to them find with Solomon that "all is vanity and vexation of spirit." This is the most favourable course of the selfish feelings, when successful and pleasurably excited; but when unsuccessful in their aims, and painfully excited, then they seem to diffuse a poison throughout the whole system, to darken the mind and impair the bodily health. Unsuccessful Love, betrayed or slighted Friendship, blighted Ambition, &c., and the host of ill-feelings and passions they raise up, such as envy, hatred, malice, jealousy, anger, fear, grief, all act injuriously on the bodily system. Each passion or sentiment has its own way of affecting the body, as it is painfully or pleasurably excited. Pale with fear, sick with love, and other similar modes of expression are not merely metaphorical, any more than, affections of the heart, bowels of compassion, the breathlessness of surprise, and so on, but are all truly indicative of parts or functions of the body intimately affected by mental states. The circulation, the digestion, the heart, the liver, the kidneys, are all influenced and disturbed under the excitement of passion or strong emotion. These functions also when disturbed *re-act* upon the mind. Thus Dr. Reid says, "He whose disposition to goodness can resist the influence of dyspepsia, and whose career of philanthropy is not liable to be checked by an obstruction in the hepatic organs, may boast of much deeper and firmer virtue than falls to the ordinary lot of human nature." The propensities are all liable to increase in activity till they become passions, and the temperature of passion is too hot to allow of the existence, much less the growth and healthy development, of the numerous small, quiet, but not the less necessary daily virtues. Any object of desire, when such desire amounts to passion,—the etymology of which word is suffering,—whether successful or unsuccessful, wears both mind and body. Hope and fear are then alternatively so strong that we may bid farewell to all mental tranquility; and when want of success brings disappointment health gives way, and the springs of life are poisoned. On the contrary, a very different state of both body and mind attends the activity of the unselfish feelings. When they habitually predominate, a constant and almost unvarying cheerfulness is the result—a cheerfulness which no grief or trouble or misfortune can long depress. Mind and body then work smoothly together, and the good or bad events that fortune brings upon us are felt according to the qualities that *we*, not *they*, possess. The subjective overpowers the objective, and such persons are said to be constitutionally happy. Poets and Philosophers all bear witness to this habitually sunshiny cast of mind; thus Pope says:

> "What nothing earthly gives, or can destroy,
> The soul's calm sunshine and the heartfelt joy,
> Is virtue's prize."

"Love, hope, and joy," says Haller, "promote perspiration, quicken the pulse, promote the circulation, and facilitate the cure of diseases." "A constant serenity, supported by hope, or cheerfulness arising from a good conscience, is the most healthful of all affections of the mind," says Dr. Mackenzie; and again, Dr. Sweetzer observes, "Let me remark, that all those mental avocations which are founded in benevolence, or whose end or aim are the good of mankind, being from their very nature associated with agreeable moral excitement, and but little mingled with the evil feelings of the heart, as envy, jealousy, hatred, must necessarily diffuse a kindly influence throughout the constitution."

If we trust to find our happiness in the indulgence of the selfish feelings, even if successful in our aims, the happiness is but transient, and as life advances we find only vacuity or disappointment, and our way to the tomb is cold, dark, joyless, and merely vegetative. On the contrary, where the moral, the æsthetic feelings, have been duly cultivated and predominate, happiness, not so intense perhaps, but more enduring,—calm, tranquil, and serene, increases as we grow older; passion has ceased, the propensities are all quiet or under due control, health and contentment reign in body and mind, and at last in "the soul's calm sunshine" we fall asleep.

The object then of moral training is the habitual predominance and activity of the higher and unselfish feelings; and we cannot begin this most important portion of Education too early.

F. CALDICOTT, PRINTER, EARL STREET, COVENTRY.

www.ingramcontent.com/pod-product-compliance
Lightning Source LLC
Chambersburg PA
CBHW030850270326
41928CB00008B/1298

* 9 7 8 3 7 4 1 1 4 1 2 8 7 *